Way Error Rebellion

A Call for Course Correction

Copyright © – Courtney Laird – 2025

All rights reserved

ISBN: 978-0-6488463-5-2

All rights reserved. No part of this publication may be reproduced, stored in a retrieval system, or transmitted in any form or by any means mechanical, electronic, photocopying or otherwise without the express written permission of the author.

The author can be contacted at:

courtney.a.laird@gmail.com

Scripture references are taken from:

The Authorised King James version of the Bible

The New King James version of the Bible © 1982 Thomas Nelson. Inc. Used by permission. All rights reserved.

Words of scripture written in bold are used by the writer for specific emphasis.

Dedication

This book is dedicated to the worldwide bride of Christ. Whilst within this text there is clear personnel application, throughout the preparation of this text I have continually felt from the Lord that this is message that He wants the bride to hear corporately. One of my greatest desires is to see the Church, the bride of Christ, walk in the fulness of the call that she has been given, and it is my prayer that what I have felt the Lord speak to me in the proceeding pages may in some small way help her to fulfill that call.

Contents

Introduction	1
Gone in the Way of Cain	13
Ran Greedily after the Error of Balaam	43
Perished in the Rebellion of Korah	75
Way Error Rebellion	93
The Two Houses	111
Final Comments	119
Bibliography	121

Introduction

This text was birthed as I was reading over and meditating on the New Testament book of Jude. At the beginning of this small yet powerful book we read of an unmistakable call to the Church, the bride of Christ, for purity in its walk:

> *Beloved, when I gave all diligence to write unto you of the common salvation, it was needful for me to write unto you, and exhort you* **that ye should earnestly contend for the faith** *which was once delivered unto the saints. (Jud 1:3) KJV*

The imploration of Jude was for his readers to earnestly contend for the faith which had once been delivered. Notice the language used here. Jude didn't just tell them to contend for the faith, but to **earnestly contend for** the faith that they had received. The Greek word for "earnestly contend for" in this passage means "to struggle for" and it is used nowhere else in the New Testament. Jude was calling his readers to engage in a struggle to hold onto the foundational truths that they had received. This was a call to action! This was not a passive statement, but one that demanded action on the part of those who read and heard it. Jude was calling the Church, and the believers who comprised it, to fight to hold on to the purity of faith that they had originally received. It was a call to hold on to and to keep holding on to. The Church and the people in it could not afford to let go of and subsequently drift away from the foundational truths that they had once received.

The connotations of this imploration of Jude bring to mind the imagery of Jacob wrestling with the angel in Genesis 32. There we read that Jacob wrestled with an angel all night, with Jacob continually holding on to and refusing to let the angel go. Such was the level of Jacobs contending that he was not willing to let go of the angel even when his hip was wrenched out of its socket. Jacob continued to hold tight and to hold strong in spite of his circumstances, in spite of his pain and in spite of the duration of the wrestle. He held strong! I believe that Jude was calling his readers to the same sort of struggle. He was calling them to hold tightly to the foundational truths that they had been taught. They needed to hold tight, they needed to wrestle, they needed to earnestly contend for and make sure that they didn't let go of the foundational truths that they had received and knew. They needed to hold onto these with the same kind of fortitude that Jacob had.

As we progress in the book of Jude, we discover why he felt so impassioned to write and implore his readers to contend for the faith:

> **For certain men have crept in unnoticed**, *who long ago were marked out for this condemnation*, **ungodly men, who turn the grace of our God into lewdness and deny the only Lord God and our Lord Jesus Christ.** *(Jud 1:4) NKJV*

The Greek word for "crept in" means to "to *settle in alongside*, that is, *lodge* stealthily". These individuals had come in the side door so to speak and lodged stealthily alongside the believers in the Church. They had not come through the front door, but sneakily came in the side, undetected. These individuals had corrupted beliefs which they sought to spread and corrupt others with. These were individuals who were in the Church, they were professing believers, but their hearts and actions showed that they had wandered from the foundational truths. Whilst professing Christ, the fruit of their lives showed that they were not aligned with the truth of the gospel. They were actually off course, and they sought to influence others to the same path.

Jude's letter was written to a Church and the believers who comprised it. This was a Church that had been birthed in the foundational truths of the gospel but had influencers come in who were seeking to take the Church away from these. The Church was at a crossroads. Whichever way it went it would still be a Church comprised of believers, but its choice would dictate whether it was a Church walking in alignment with the truths of the Word or a Church that wasn't. The choice that the Church made in response to Jude's letter would dictate whether this would be a Church that was on fire for the Lord or whether it would be a Church that was lukewarm.

We see here the same battle that has plagued the Church since its birth, the battle of truth against deception. The enemy always comes to try and lead the people of God away from the truth of God through subtle deception. He did it with Adam and Eve and he still does it today. He will always seek to question the truth of the Word in order to introduce deception. It is a little leaven the leavens the whole lump and as believers we need to be wary of the leaven of the enemies tactics.

In Jude we see a negative influence seeking to infiltrate the Church. Jude is about the condition of the Church and about the believers within it needing to ensure that their trajectory is still in line with the foundational truths of the Word of the Lord. It highlights the need for believers to be like the Berean people spoken about in the book of Acts and always make sure that our path completely aligns with the truths of scripture (Acts 17:11). It is a call to purity.

What is interesting to note is that this was not the message that Jude had originally intended to write (Jude 1:3). Jude had originally intended to write unto the Church about the common salvation. The Lord though impressed upon him the need to change his plans. There was something more pressing that the Lord wanted the Church to hear. There was an infiltration that had occurred and had to be addressed. The Lord had a message that the Church needed to here!

As I read over the epistle and considered the individuals Jude was referring to, the Lord began to continually highlight one particular verse to me:

> *Woe to them! For they have gone in the way of Cain, have run greedily in the error of Balaam for profit, and perished in the rebellion of Korah. (Jud 1:11) NKJV*

INTRODUCTION

As I read, reread and mediated upon this verse the Lord started to speak a message to my heart.

In describing the individuals who were having a negative influence upon the Church Jude used a lot of descriptive and symbolic language. Jude referred to them as clouds without water, spots at their feasts, raging waves of the sea and fruitless trees to name a few. In the verse above Jude directly compared this group to three specific individuals from the Old Testament: Cain, Balaam and Korah. As I sought the Lord on this and what it meant, I felt the Lord say that whilst these are three specific individuals listed this is also a reference to three specific spirits that seek to come against the Church and the people of God. These are spirits of influence that seek to draw the people of God away from the truth. There is a spirit of Cain, a spirit of Balaam and a spirit of Korah that war against the people of God, the Church and seek to draw them from the foundational truths.

To try and expound upon this thought and explain it better, in the book of 1 and 2 Kings we read about a woman named Jezebel. From scripture we are given great insights into the character and nature of this woman. We know her to be a callous individual and one who particularly warred against the prophets of God. She was the violent, idolatrous wife of king Ahab and had a personal vendetta against the prophet Elijah. Whilst we know that this was an actual historical individual, most of us as believers would also be aware or have a knowledge of the spirit of Jezebel. There is the woman and there is the spirit behind the woman. It is with this understanding that when we come to the book of Revelation we can rightly interpret Rev 2:20:

> *Nevertheless I have a few things against you, because you allow* ***that woman Jezebel****, who calls herself a prophetess, to teach and seduce My servants to commit sexual immorality and eat things sacrificed to idols. (Rev 2:20) NKJV*

The reference here is not to another woman named Jezebel who just happened to share the same characteristics as the Jezebel of the Old Testament. Jesus was addressing the spirit of Jezebel that was at work in the Church of Thyatira seeking to corrupt and draw the Church away from foundational truths it had been birthed in. It is the same spirit of Jezebel upon a different individual but operating with the exact same characteristics and motives as were evident in the Old Testament individual. It is the same spirit again, warring against the Church and the people of God.

From scripture we see that there was the woman Jezebel and then there is the spirit behind the woman, the spirit of Jezebel. It is the character and the actions of the individual that give us as believers insights into the spirit behind them. There is the individual and there is the spirit behind them.

I would suggest that the same situation exists in this passage of Jude. There are the individuals of Cain, Balaam and Korah and then there are the spirits of Cain, Balaam and Korah. It was these three spirits that were seeking to come against the early Church and draw the Church away from the truths of the Word. In my opinion these same spirits still run rife today and still seek to draw the Church and the people of God away from her foundational truths.

Just as with Jezebel though, in order for us to understand these spirits and how they operate, we need to first understand biblically the character, nature and actions of these men. That is, to understand the spirits of Cain, Balaam and Korah we must first have a biblical understanding of the men themselves. It is first the natural and then the spiritual (1 Cor 15:46). It is as we gain an understanding of these individuals that we arm ourselves to be able to identify and resist the spirits associated with them and their influence on the Church.

Our Approach

Our focus for this text will be on Jude 1:11:

> *Woe to them! For they have gone in the way of Cain, have run greedily in the error of Balaam for profit, and perished in the rebellion of Korah. (Jud 1:11) NKJV*

INTRODUCTION

If we break down this verse, we can see that there are three parts to it:

1. Gone in the Way of Cain
2. Ran greedily after the Error of Balaam
3. Perished in the Rebellion of Korah

In scripture the number three is symbolic of God and of perfect witness. In the use of the three examples of these individuals by Jude we have the perfect witness of their true state.

Jude doesn't just reference three random individuals though; he very clearly and descriptively makes the comparison that he is making known by providing us with enough detail to readily identify each individual from scripture.

If we zoom in a little more on what we have already broken down of Jude 1:11, within this threefold reference of Jude, we can also see a repeated triplet of parts. It is three within three. As we examine these parts, we can see that each reference has a recurring triplet of **action, path** and **individual**. The individuals Jude was referring to had:

Gone in the Way of Cain
Ran greedily after the Error of Balaam
Perished in the Rebellion of Korah

Jude describes the actions of these individuals as having gone, having ran and having perished. He describes their path as way, error and rebellion and finally he lists the individuals as Cain, Balaam and Korah. Each of the three references has an individual, an action and a path:

Action	Path	Individual
Gone	Way	Cain
Ran	Error	Balaam
Perished	Rebellion	Korah

It is these recuring parts of individual, action and path that will form the structure of our study moving forward. As we investigate each of these references to learn more about the spirits they refer to, we will look at the individual, their path, and their action before we then consider how the influence that each of these spirits has upon the Church and believers today may look. We will then close each section with some questions to help us take on honest reflective introspection on the spiritual state of our lives and Churches.

The Application

At the core of this epistle of Jude is a message not just to the Church that Jude was writing to all those years ago, but a message to **The Church**, worldwide from Jude's time unto ours. Just as the message of Jesus to the Churches in Revelation has just as much application today so too does the message of Jude. The great reality is that the enemies' tactics have never really changed and one of his greatest tools is to try and pull the people of God away from the truth of the Word.

It would be foolish and arrogant for us to think that the pressures and spiritual influences that came against the early Church do not still try and come against the Church today. It is often said that the biggest lesson that we learn from history is that we never learn from history. Rather than learn from past experiences, we at times seem to think of ourselves as incapable of repeating the same mistakes as those who have gone before us only to find that in hindsight that is exactly what we have done.

INTRODUCTION

The epistle of Jude is one that we as the Church must learn from. We must understand the message that Jude was writing to the Church so that we can learn from it and not repeat the same mistakes. This is not meant to be a study of judgement or come across as condemnatory in any way, but rather it is intended to be a study of observation, introspection and encouragement for us to take hold of the truths of the epistle of Jude and be the Church that we have been called to be. As the people of God rather than just brush off Jude's message as inapplicable, we must always be able to openly and honestly look at this message and ask ourselves:

- Have we wandered from the foundational truths of the Gospel?

- Have we let ourselves be influenced by the way of Cain, the error of Balaam and the rebellion of Korah?

- Have these influences gradually changed our course, and are we now at the point where we must earnestly contend for the faith one delivered and make a course correction?

If we as the Church have let ourselves be influenced by these spirits and wandered from the foundational truths, whether that be intentionally or accidently, we will find ourselves in a new norm that is outside the perfect path of the Father.

In this season I believe that the Lord is wanting us to honestly examine our true state. There is a call of the Spirit for the Church to earnestly contend for and return to the foundational truths upon which it was built. The Lord is sending out a call of purity unto the bride and is calling her to have an ear to hear what the Spirit would say (Rev 2:7, 17).

As we move forward, I would ask that you maintain a teachable spirit as you consider and meditate upon that which is presented. That is by no means saying that you should automatically adopt everything written within the following pages as pure truth. I am more than aware of my own inadequacies with trying to convey that which I have felt the Lord speak and you may not necessarily agree with everything that is written. There may be however just one line within this text that the Lord would have you to hear and if you hear it, then this text has served its purpose. This text may not change your life, but it may allow the Lord to deposit one nugget of gold.

As we progress, we will examine both a number of biblical quotes and references. My encouragement would be for you to read over these to make sure that what has been written **completely aligns** with the Word of God.

Before we move any further would you join me in praying:

> *Lord as I read over the pages of this study, I ask that if there is anything within it that you need or that you want me to hear, would you please soften my heart, quicken my spirit and allow me to receive that which you have for me. Would you protect me from any error of man, be it the authors, mine or things I have been taught, and would you allow the truth of your Word to sink in deeply.*
>
> *Lord, would you remove from me now any preconceived prejudice or walls that I may have and would you allow me to be moulded by you and your Word. I give you permission to shape me with your truth.*
>
> *Holy Spirit, would you please speak to my spirit that which you have for me and help me to maintain a teachable spirit as a noble Berean.*
>
> *In Jesus name,*
>
> *Amen.*

It is my sincere prayer that you hear that which the Lord would have for you, however little or much that may be, and that together we become the Church that the Lord is calling us to be.

Blessings in Christ,

The Way of Cain

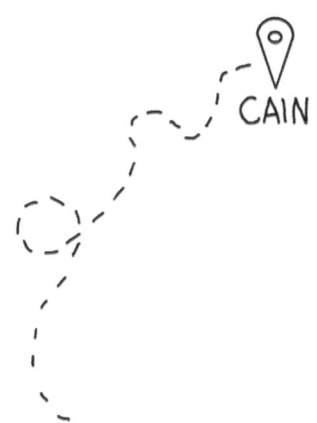

Gone in the Way of Cain

Woe to them! **For they have gone in the way of Cain**, *have run greedily in the error of Balaam for profit, and perished in the rebellion of Korah. (Jud 1:11) NKJV*

The Individual

We are first introduced to Cain in Genesis 4 where we are told that Cain was the firstborn son of Adam and Eve. Cain was actually the first human to be born on the earth! Cain then became a brother as Adam and Eve had another son, Abel. As these two grew up we read that Abel became a keeper of the flock and Cain was a tiller of the ground. Whilst we understand that these roles refer to Abel being a shepherd and Cain a farmer or husbandmen, we get some further insights into these men when we look at the definition of the Hebrew words used for these roles.

With Abel, the word for "keeper" of the flock according to Strongs Concordance means: "to *tend* a flock, that is, *pasture* it; intransitively to *graze* (literally or figuratively); generally to *rule*; by extension to *associate* with (as a friend)". The word carries with it a sense of overseeing and being responsible for what is under an individual's care. Abel literally oversaw the flock and tended to its needs.

On the other hand the word for "tiller", as used in reference to Cain, means "to *work* (in any sense); by implication to *serve, till*, (causatively) *enslave*, etc". This word carries with it the sense of bondage and enslavement. Cain, as a tiller, served the ground, he was enslaved to it. This is the first insight that we get into Cain as a person.

In Genesis 4 we read that in the process of time both Cain and Abel came before the Lord with an offering. Cain brought forth the fruit of the ground that he had worked for. Abel though brought of the firstlings from his flock, those that he looked after and that he cared for. As both of these offerings were presented before the Lord, we read that the Lord looked with respect upon Abel and upon his offering, but He did not look with respect upon Cain or his offering. It is here we get a further insight into Cain. Instead of Godly repentance forming in Cain because of this, we read that anger arouse in Cain and his countenance changed. There was a jealousy within Cain in regards to how the Lord had looked upon Abel's offering compared to how the Lord had looked upon his. This highlights to us the comparative and competitive nature of Cain and also the pride within him.

Having seen Cain's response, the Lord came and spoke to him:

> *So the LORD said to Cain, "Why are you angry? And why has your countenance fallen? If you do well, will you not be accepted? And if you do not do well, sin lies at the door. And its desire is for you, but you should rule over it." (Gen 4:6-7) NKJV*

The Lord started the conversation by asking Cain "why are you angry and why has your countenance changed?" We see here that the Lord immediately addressed Cain's inner emotions and also the effects that they were having upon Cain outwardly. The Lord already knew the answer to this question just as He knew the answers to the questions He asked of Adam in Genesis 3! The questions of the Lord here were for not for the Lord's curiosity but rather for Cain's benefit. The Lord was trying to drill down and get Cain to admit what was going on. He was attempting to start a conversation that could lead to healing. From what we go on to read we can probably safely assume that Cain was not willing to engage with what the Lord was trying to do here.

The Lord then addressed the issue at the heart of the matter by saying "I know what is upsetting you but if you do well shall you not be accepted". It is my belief that the deep seeded anger within Cain was already arousing within him thoughts and actions that he wanted to carry out against his brother. The words of the Lord here were really a warning. "If you do well... **BUT** if you don't, sin lies at the door". In other words, Cain you have a decision to make. You know what is right and you know what is wrong (Gen 3:5). The Lord was gently leading Cain to a place where he had the opportunity to repent and change his way.

As we continue in Genesis 4 it would seem that Cain ignored these interactions with the Lord as after talking with his brother Abel, Cain rose up and killed him.

> *Now Cain talked with Abel his brother; and it came to pass, when they were in the field, that Cain rose up against Abel his brother and killed him. (Gen 4:8) NKJV*

This was the first murder committed on the earth! Cain become the first person to kill someone, and Abel become the first martyr, an individual who was killed because of their faith.

Cain's issue lay not so much in that Abel's offering was accepted, but rather that his wasn't. Pride can be seen at the heart of Cain. The Hebrew word used in regard to Cain killing Able in verse 8 means "to smite with deadly intent". This action was not accidental on the part of Cain. It was not a situation that had gotten out of hand. Cain struck his brother with deadly intent. There was deliberate and purposeful intent to what Cain did!

After this, the Lord again came to Cain and gave him the opportunity to engage in restorative communication. The Lord asked Cain where his brother was. Again, the Lord knew what had happened. This question was not for the Lord's benefit, but Cain's. Note though the childishness in the response of Cain. "I don't know, I am not my brother keeper". This statement shows a complete lack of respect and honour for who Cain was talking to. It is like the shrug of an insolent teenager.

The Lord then told Cain that He knew exactly what had happened and He pronounced His judgement on Cain for his sin and his complete lack of repentance for it. Throughout all of this, Cain expressed no remorse for what he had done, his only concern was for himself. He protested to the Lord that his punishment was too harsh and that he might be killed living as a vagabond. He had no problem rising against his brother, but was afraid at the thought that someone might possibly do the same thing to him under the punishment of the Lord.

Through this short account we see that Cain exhibits pride, anger, envy, jealousy, unrepentance, self-focus and selfishness. He is an individual consumed with self. Having considered the individual let us consider now what the Way of Cain is.

The Path

*Gone in the **Way of Cain**. (Jude 1:11) NKJV*

When we come to considering what the way of Cain that Jude is referring to is, there are three distinct interactions that we need to examine in the life of Cain. These are Cain's interaction with sacrifice, Cain's interaction with Abel and finally Cain's interaction with the Lord. Each of these interactions reveal to us facets of what the way of Cain looks like.

CAIN'S INTERACTION WITH SACRIFICE AND WORSHIP.

The first point for us to consider centres around Cain's approach unto the Lord and what he presented to Him. Before we jump more fully into this, there are two things that we must be aware of in regard to worship in Cain's time. Our points here are adapted from another text I have written as they deal directly with what we are considering:

1. God had already revealed the standard for sacrificial worship.

In Genesis 3 we read of the fall of man when Adam and Eve ate of the forbidden fruit. When Adam and Eve partook, we are told that their eyes were opened, and they realised that they were both naked. To hide their nakedness, Adam and Eve sowed fig leaves together and made coverings for themselves. Later though, the Lord came to the garden and after Adam and Eve had admitted their transgression, the Lord pronounced a sentence upon them and the serpent for what had happened. After the Lord has pronounced His judgement, He did one final thing for Adam and Eve. In Genesis 3:21 we read:

> *Unto Adam also and to his wife did the LORD God make coats of skins, and clothed them. (Gen 3:21) KJV*

The question we need to consider here is why did the Lord make Adam and Eve coats of skins? Adam and Eve had already covered their nakedness with the fig leaves they had sown together! The fig leaves though were a man made covering and the truth revealed is that man's efforts can never cover the consequences of sin. God took away that which man had created to cover his sin and instead gave unto him coats of skin, a Godly covering that had come from the death of a substitute victim. An animal was killed for the coats to be given, but the animal wasn't killed for the sole purpose of providing clothing. The animals were killed because as the book of Hebrews tells us the only thing that can take away the stain of sin is blood.

> *And according to the law almost all things are purified with blood,* **and without shedding of blood there is no remission***. (Heb 9:22) NKJV*

The coats of skin that came from the Lord revealed to Adam and Eve His sacrificial system of atonement. The only means of atonement for sin is that of the death of a substitute victim and the provision of innocent blood. In this instance God himself set forth for Adam and Eve the sacrifice and having atoned for their sins, He clothed them with coats of redemption. God cleansed, He covered, and He demonstrated unto Adam and Eve how He was to be approached in worship. Here God set forth His standard for sacrificial worship.

2. The Ground had been cursed.

Genesis 4 tells us that Cain was a tiller of the ground and that it was from what he produced through his efforts in this that Cain brough forth fruit as an offering unto the Lord.

> *Then she bore again, this time his brother Abel. Now Abel was a keeper of sheep,* **but Cain was a tiller of the ground**. *And in the process of time it came to pass that* **Cain brought an offering of the fruit of the ground** *to the* LORD. *(Gen 4:2-3)* NKJV

A chapter earlier in Genesis 3 though, we read that as part of the judgement upon Adam and Eve for their sin, God had cursed the ground:

> *Then to Adam He said, "Because you have heeded the voice of your wife, and have eaten from the tree of which I commanded you, saying, 'You shall not eat of it':* **"Cursed is the ground for your sake; In toil you shall eat of it All the days of your life.** *Both thorns and thistles it shall bring forth for you, And you shall eat the herb of the field.* **In the sweat of your face you shall eat bread** *Till you return to the ground, For out of it you were taken; For dust you are, And to dust you shall return." (Gen 3:17-19)* NKJV

When Adam and Eve sinned, God cursed the ground. It would not only produce good plants, but it would now also produce thorns and thistles. Further to this, rather than the ground readily bringing forth its fruit for man to eat, it would require effort and sweat on the part of man to produce a crop. In other words, growing fruit and vegetables was going to be hard work. Cain would have worked hard to produce that which he brought unto the Lord. He had to work the ground and protect his crops from thorns and weeds. This was all done through the sweat, toil and effort of Cain. As we touched on earlier in our look at the word 'tiller', Cain had to serve the ground to get the produce that he wanted.

The two points we have considered above are things that both Cain and Abel would have known. Their knowledge base and experience would have been exactly the same and yet despite this, their ways are completely different. Why was this? Why did Cain bring an offering of the fruit of the ground even though he knew this was not the right approach? Why not just ask Abel for one of the flock? It would be my suggestion that the answer to these questions are that Cain's understanding and motivation for worship was fundamentally flawed.

When it came to bringing an offering unto the Lord, Cain chose to ignore the way of approach that the Lord Himself had revealed unto his parents, Adam and Eve, and instead, Cain chose to come unto the Lord through the efforts of the flesh. Cain chose to bring unto the Lord from the fruit of the ground. Remember, as we discovered above, the ground had been cursed at the fall! That which Cain brought he had to labour and sweat for. Cains worship was based in works. He chose to approach the Lord with that which made him feel like he had sacrificed. His sacrifice was based on how he felt and not how it made the Lord feel. It was a self-pleasing fleshy worship. Cain felt like he had sacrificed because what he brought was the results of his efforts. He no doubt looked with pride on that which he had toiled and grown and set before the Lord. The flesh of Cain was satisfied by what he had done and by what he had presented unto the Lord.

Cain chose a different way to Abel. Cain chose the way that made him feel good about sacrifice and worship. Cain was essentially saying to the Lord: "this is how I will worship you. I am setting aside the way you have directed because this way, the one that I have chosen, makes me feel good and this makes me feel like I have sacrificed. I feel good worshipping you in this way therefore this is how I will approach. I am choosing to step aside from the truth of my father and approach my own way". It was an approach based on what Cain got out of worship and how it made Cain feel.

With Cain what we see is a flesh-based approach to sacrifice and worship. It is a form of honouring God that has the appearance of being right, but it is an approach whose focus is solely on the satisfaction of self. Cain chose to set aside the truth that the Lord had given unto Adam and Eve and chose his own way. He chose to approach the Lord in a way that satisfied him. It was the way of self-satisfying worship. It was an approach that was rooted in the satisfaction of the flesh rather than in the glorification of God. It was self-focused rather than God focused. Cain's approach was one rooted in self and flesh.

It is for this reason that God could not look upon his offering with respect. God can never bless that which is rooted in disobedience.

CAINS INTERACTION WITH ABEL.

And Now Cain talked with Abel his brother; and it came to pass, when they were in the field, that Cain rose up against Abel his brother and killed him. (Gen 4:8) NKJV

The next point for us to consider is that of Cain's interaction with Abel. It is interesting to note that the pride of Cain did not allow him to talk to his brother prior to the time of sacrifice to possibly ask for one of the flock to sacrifice! No doubt at times other members of the family had approached Abel in regard to this! The pride of Cain though had to show that the way in which he approached was a better way. His way, his works were superior. This, as we know, was not the case though! In Genesis we are told that the Lord looked with respect upon the offering of Abel, but not on Cain's. But what does this mean? How did Cain know that the Lord had looked with respect on Abel's offering but not his? How was he able to discern this? When we look through the Word of God, we see that throughout scripture the Lord has always shows His acceptance of sacrifice with fire.

> *Then the fire of the LORD fell and consumed the burnt sacrifice, and the wood and the stones and the dust, and it licked up the water that was in the trench. (1Ki 18:38) NKJV*

> *and fire came out from before the LORD and consumed the burnt offering and the fat on the altar. When all the people saw it, they shouted and fell on their faces. (Lev 9:24) NKJV*

> *(see also: Judges 6:22, Acts 2:3).*

I would put forth, on the balance of scriptural interpretation, that this is what happened here. The respect of the Lord was shown through the holy fire of the Lord consuming Abel's sacrifice but not Cain's. Abel saw it and Cain would have seen it too. It was actually this acceptance of the Lord towards Abel's offering that caused the reaction in Cain. If Abel hadn't presented an offering, or the acceptance of the Lord wasn't clear and visible, I would suggest that there would have been no such reaction in Cain. Abel's offering though showed the insufficiency of what Cain had brought unto the Lord and it was this that caused the reaction in Cain. Cain believed that his way was better and did not want his way to feel inferior to Abel's. We see here that within Cain self reacted.

After seeing the acceptance of Abel's offering, Cain suddenly wanted to talk with his brother. What did Cain possibly want to talk about? We know that the Lord had already warned Cain that sin was lying at the door and that he had a choice to make, so his motivation in this conversation was most likely not from a good place. The actions of Cain post conversation further confirm this as we read that Cain rose against his brother and killed him. How quickly the conversation turned to violence!

What we see here is the age-old battle of the flesh versus the spirit.

> *For the flesh lusts against the Spirit, and the Spirit against the flesh; and these are contrary to one another, so that you do not do the things that you wish. (Gal 5:17) NKJV*

> *(See Also Rom 8:1-13, Gal 4:29)*

The way of the flesh in worship does not like to be shown up by the way of the Spirit in approaching the Lord. The Spirit caused a reaction to the flesh of Cain, it provoked it and caused the fruit of the flesh to be seen in Cain. With Cain we see a desire of the flesh to quench the worship done in Spirit and truth. Why? Because true worship, that which Abel offered, does not satisfy self and this causes the flesh to react. The flesh always wants satisfaction. The Spirit agitates the flesh and so in response the flesh seeks to make its way of approach as the only way of approach. As the flesh against the Spirit, so was Cain against Abel.

Cain sought to persuade, intimidate and change Abel's approach with words and when that didn't work, he lashed out and sought to completely shut down the ability of Abel to worship and approach the Lord in Spirit. The flesh shut down the Spirit.

CAINS INTERACTION WITH THE LORD.

As we look at this point, it is worthy for us to be reminded that Cain had a clear relationship with the Lord. In our Christian way of thinking we can often play Cain and Abel against each other and look at Abel as having a relationship with the Lord, but Cain not so much. This isn't the case though! Both Abel and Cain had a relationship with the Lord, Abel's was just deeper! Cain sought to approach the Lord, Cain heard from the Lord, and Cain spoke with the Lord. These are the characteristics of someone who is in relationship with the Lord! These are the characteristics that we would associate with a modern-day Christian!

Within the passage from Genesis 4 there are two conversations, or interactions, that the Lord had with Cain. The first was a word of warning to Cain from the Lord which Cain seemed to ignore (Gen 4:6-7). He heard the Lord but didn't act upon the word of admonition. The second conversation was a little more intense as the Lord came and questioned Cain. The Lord opened the door for Cain to repent, but when Cain rebuffed the Lord, that door shut, and the Lord declared His judgment upon Cain. Note the two responses of Cain to this conversation, highlighted below:

> *Then the LORD said to Cain, "Where is Abel your brother?"* **He said, "I do not know. Am I my brother's keeper?"** *And He said, "What have you done? The voice of your brother's blood cries out to Me from the ground. So now you are cursed from the earth, which has opened its mouth to receive your brother's blood from your hand. When you till the ground, it shall no longer yield its strength to you. A fugitive and a vagabond you shall be on the earth."* **And Cain said to the LORD, "My punishment is greater than I can bear! Surely You have driven me out this day from the face of the ground; I shall be hidden from Your face; I shall be a fugitive and a vagabond on the earth, and it will happen that anyone who finds me will kill me."** *And the LORD said to him, "Therefore, whoever kills Cain, vengeance shall be taken on him sevenfold." And the LORD set a mark on Cain, lest anyone finding him should kill him. (Gen 4:9-15) NKJV*

The responses of Cain in this passage reveal two things to us about Cain's relationship with the Lord:

1. Cain had **NO** fear of the Lord.

Cain's initial response to the Lord is one of complete insolence, "I don't know, am I my brother's keeper?" Cain was speaking to the Lord, the very one whom just a few verses ago he had sought to bring an offering too to show off his piety. His response though shows the true nature of Cain's relationship with the Lord. It was one devoid of any fear of the Lord. Cain initially completely ignored the corrective warning of the Lord and then he had the audacity to speak back to Him like a rebellious teenager.

Psalm 111:10 tells us that the fear of the Lord is the beginning of wisdom. The Hebrew word for beginning in this verse means "in place, time, order or rank (specifically a *firstfruit*)". The fear of the

Lord is the first building block for wisdom in the life of any believer. It is the starting point of wisdom. Cain did not have any fear of the Lord! He had not even started on the path of wisdom. Cain's lack of reverential fear highlights to us the infantile nature and the immaturity of his relationship with the Lord. Cain was a babe in the faith and whilst he had grown up naturally and physically, spiritually there had not been the same growth as there had been in his brother Abel. Cain's relationship with the Lord was one of spiritual immaturity and stagnation.

2. The self-consumption of Cain.

Cains relationship with the Lord was simply based on what he got out of it. It was completely one sided. Note that at no stage do we read of any repentance from Cain over his sacrifice not being accepted. There was no conviction that what he had offered did not measure up to the Lord's standards. There was no remorse that his offering fell short of what God would accept. His spirit was not wounded, only his pride by what had happened.

We also do not see any repentance from Cain in regard to his actions against his brother or in regard to his terse response to the Lord. Cain's only concern was over how the judgement of the Lord for his actions was going to affect his own life. It is the response of an unrepentant child who has been caught in the wrong but doesn't want to accept the consequences. It is a response rooted in the interests of self. Cain had no remorse over killing his brother, but fears that someone may do the same to him!

Cain relationship was one where the Lord was supposed to serve him and meet his needs. It is a self-based relationship that sees the Lord as a genie in a bottle who is there to grant our every wish.

Cain was an individual who had a relationship with the Lord. He approached the Lord. He worshipped the Lord. He talked and engaged with the Lord. The fire of the Lord though was not present in this relationship. It was a relationship that was based in immaturity and one that was lacking intimacy.

From our consideration of the above points, we can summarise that with the way of Cain we see:

> A relationship and approach unto the Lord that is based in the flesh. Cain's motivation was ruled by how it made him feel and what he got out of it. It was a satisfaction of self at the expense of the glorification of God. The result of this approach was that Cain's relationship and worship were devoid of the fire of the Lord. His experience of the Lord was far less than that of his brother because his behaviour was rooted in the satisfaction of his flesh.

$$\text{Satisfaction} > \text{Glorification}$$

> A pride in his own approach as being the preeminent way of approaching the Lord. Subsequently when this was shown to not be the case, rather than repent we see a reaction that sought to dissuade and extinguish true worship. The pride of Cain meant that he was unwilling and unable to humble himself and thus the only solution was to dispose of that which demonstrated and highlighted the insufficiency of his way.

> An immaturity in his walk with the Lord because of a lack of reverential fear. It is a selfish one-sided relationship that seeks the blessings and favour of God without ever giving anything out. It is a meet my needs relationship that is comfortable with feeling good in its approach rather than pursuing the fire of God. It is the mark of a relationship with the Lord that has stagnated and not matured.

Possibly the worst thing about the way of Cain is summed up for us in Gen 4:9 where we see the culmination of the way:

> *And **Cain went out from the presence of the LORD**,*
> *and dwelt in the land of Nod, on the east of Eden. (Gen 4:16)*
> KJV

Rather than coming into the presence of the Lord, Cain went out from it! The way of Cain led him in the opposite direction to the presence of the Lord. The saddest thing is that we never read of Cain ever returning!

The Action

> *Woe unto them! for they have **gone** in the way of Cain, (Jud 1:11) NKJV*

Jude says that the individuals he was referring to had **GONE** in the way of Cain. The word for 'gone' here is the Greek word "poreuomai" and it means: "to *traverse*, that is, *travel* (literally or figuratively; especially to *remove* [figuratively *die*], *live*, etc.)". In scripture it is translated as: "depart, go (away, forth, one's way, up), (make a, take a) journey, walk".

At the core of this action is a choice. A choice to travel, a choice to depart, a choice to go a specific way. It is a decision by the individual to take a specific course; it is not accidental.

What is clear from our look at Genesis 4 is that there were only two ways. There was the way of Cain or the Way of Abel. In all reality we could better define it as the way of man and the way of God.

The individuals Jude was referring to had made the choice to go in the way of Cain, the way of man. These individuals had chosen to depart from the right way, the way of God, the way of Abel. It is as if they had stood at a fork in the road and consciously chosen which way to take.

The question is why? Why would they do this? For the same reasons as Cain did!

With this action what we see is a first step, but not a last step! The way of Cain is a moving away from the truth of the Word and choosing to approach the Lord in a way that pleases the flesh!

The spirit of Cain

Having looked at the way of Cain in some detail, we now turn our attention to consider what would be some indications that the spirit of Cain could be operating within our Churches just as it was in Jude's day. We, as the people of God, face the same battles and the same challenges. The enemies' tactics have not changed and as the people of God we need to be aware of them so that we too can stand and contend for the faith.

As we do this, I would encourage you that if there is anything that causes an inner reaction as you read, would you pause and seek the Lord as to why the reaction is occurring. It could be that you may not agree with what is written and that is fine, but it could also be that the Lord may be trying to reveal something to you that you may not have seen before. Either way please pray for a spirit of discernment and take the time to seek Him about it rather than just brushing it off.

The spirit of Cain could be present:

IF OUR SERVICES HAVE A FOCUS ON PRODUCTION.

If in our times of corporate worship there is a focus on lighting and smoke, on having the right speakers and having the right sound system, having the right videographer and on having the right images on the screen then that is an indicator of a focus on the flesh. It is seeking to create something that appeals and satisfies man. Whilst none of these are necessarily bad it is also true that none of these are actually necessary for the glorification of God within our services!

Over time, we as the Church have slowly adopted the ways of the world into our services and have in many cases ended up replicating an environment that is identical to a concert in the world in an effort to draw people in like moths to a flame, making worship an active experience rather than the act of sacrifice that it is intended to be. We have sought to make our services appealing to man and we justify this with comments like 'we have a responsibility to reach the next generation', 'we have to create a place where people feel comfortable' or 'we have to be relevant'. All of these things sound right from a human mindset but if our focus is on creating an atmosphere so that people can feel comfortable in how they approach the Lord then our compass is off just like Cain's was. This type of approach is focused on the individual rather than on the act they are performing. Just like Cain, it is not an absence of an approach unto the Lord, but it is one where the focus is on the satisfaction of the flesh rather than on the glorification of God. This can be the issue with so many of the things that we do. Just like Cain, the appearance seems right. We are approaching the Lord, coming before him with a "sacrifice" yet it is a sacrifice that is not according to His requirements but rather ours, and the intent behind it is completely wrong.

We need to make sure that production never becomes more important than God in our services. If the fear of the absence of production raises concerns about the effect it could have on our attendance numbers, then it may indicate that there is an underlying problem with our focus. When productions main focus is on the flesh of man then the spirit of Cain may be present.

IF OUR WORSHIP IS FOCUSED ON APPEAL.

Another great indicator for the spirit of Cain surrounds our times of worship. This includes not just the songs we sing, but the time that we give unto worship and how we let worship flow. In an effort to please our congregations and to attract new individuals we may be tempted to try and create a time of worship that appeals to man. We may set limits on the time it goes for, we may want to make sure that it is upbeat and modern, we may even restrict the flow of the Spirit so as not to make anyone feel uncomfortable. The flow on from this is that we end up developing a worship routine that is replicated each and every week. We develop our own approach in worship that we then repeat on a weekly basis. Unknowingly like Cain we end up dictating how we will approach the Lord. We move away from His way, and we adopt our own.

The worship may be loud and energetic, and we may walk away feeling pumped up by what we have brought. The problem is though that we mistakenly confuse the satisfaction of the flesh for the outpouring of the Spirit. It is only when we see the fire of the Lord descend on true worship that we ever notice that ours falls short, but rather than repenting we can tend to try and justify why our approach is right. This is what Cain did. He sought to set aside sacrifice in worship and instead make it into something that he was satisfied by and when he saw that his approach fell short, he then shut true worship down. Worship by its very nature though is sacrificial. It is something that should cost. We do not do it for what we get, we do it for He is worthy of nothing less.

Again, we should be able to identify that whilst the intentions behind our reasons for the worship that we give may sound good and indeed come from a good place, the focus of these reasons once again highlights a focus that is on the flesh. It is seeking to create an environment of worship that is satisfactory to man. It is the same mistake as Cain. It is stepping aside from the truths that God has revealed and instead choosing to approach in a way that makes man feel good.

If the theme of man ever comes up as a justification for how we do worship, it is a sign that the spirit of Cain may be present in our Church. Rather than reacting like Cain to a demonstration of true worship we have to maintain a teachable spirit so that we may change our way of approach to match the Lord's rather than mans. Our worship should appeal to God alone!

IF WE HAVE AN EXAGGERATED EMPHASIS ON THE STAGE.

Cains approach was on the satisfaction of what he got from coming before the Lord. Man was at the centre of Cain's approach rather than the Lord.

A sign of this in the modern Church can be if there is an overemphasis placed on the stage, especially when the worship is on.

The lights get turned down, the spotlights come on and if that doesn't achieve the desired effect, we can be tempted to add more lighting effects to the stage area so that people's attention and focus is drawn there. Whilst the intention may be to try and help people press into worship all that we really do is force the congregations focus to be on the ones leading worship up the front rather than on Him who is above. It is a method that literally forces man to be at the centre of our focus in worship. Rather than individuals being led into worship with a focus on our heavenly Father their focus is forced toward the entertainment that is before them.

We may well ask, why do we highlight the stage and what focus should this really have in worship? Where does this idea come from?

The biblical truth is that the role of those who lead in praise and worship is not to have the focus but rather to help direct the focus of the congregation to heaven. Whenever we force the focus to be on the stage, we actually inhibit the ability of the praise and worship team to do this. By forcing a focus upon the stage, we like Cain attempt to place a spotlight on man in worship.

An overemphasis on the stage is an indicator that the spirit of Cain may be present.

IF OUR MESSAGES ARE CONTINUALLY FOCUSED ON ENCOURAGEMENT.

Another sign that the spirit of Cain may be present is if we tend to preach with a focus of on how individuals can have a better life, how they can be blessed and how they can walk in the prosperity of the Lord and if we rarely ever preach and teach on the fear of the Lord. These types of messages are popular and will attract an audience and we can be tempted to shy away from the harder hitting elements of the gospel so as not to offend anyone. These types of messages though show that there is a focus on satisfying the flesh of the congregation rather than preaching the truth of the gospel and letting the sword of the Lord have its way in the lives of men and women. These are messages designed to appeal to the heart of man and keep the congregation happy. The primary objective of any message though should be to please God and not man.

With any message there always has to be application to the individual. I would actually go as far to say that without any application a message actually falls short of its objective. In saying that though, the focus of any message should always be on growing the individual in their relationship with the Lord and seeing them transformed further into His image. Our messages should ever be God centred and never self-centred. It is only through the refining fire of the Word that we can truly grow and be transformed further into the image of Christ.

When we water our messages down to make them palatable to an audience, we actually dilute them of the Spirit of the Lord and replace them with the flesh of man. If our messages are focused on the benefits man gets from God, then it is an indication that the spirit of Cain may be present.

IF OUR BUILDING IS FOCUSED ON PRESTIGE.

Owning a building is not a bad thing and not owning a building is not a bad thing. Buildings of any shape and size help Christian gatherings occur. The evidence of the spirit of Cain becomes apparent though when our focus shifts to the appeal of our building, its size, capacity and grandeur. Whether our building is better than the Church down the road and whether or not we need a new building so that we can keep up with Jones'.

Part of Cain's error was the grandeur that he wrongly associated with his worship. The fruit basket that Cain presented looked far nicer than the bloody mess that Abel offered. It was nicer, it was neater, and it looked more appealing. Like with Cain's offering, our buildings can unconsciously become a surrogate for the worship that we offer. We can feel good going to worship because of the place where we worship. Our building can create within us a level of satisfaction regarding our worship of the Lord. What this again highlights though is a focus on the flesh. It reveals a satisfaction of the flesh in our approach unto the Lord. We are pleased with how we approach.

The reality is that the Lord doesn't care about our buildings in terms of the worship that we offer! God looks at the heart not the structure. His focus is never on the building and nor should ours be. Such a focus highlights that the spirit of Cain may be present.

IF OUR GOAL IS THE ATTRACTION OF A CROWD, RATHER THAN THE MATURING OF A FLOCK.

In modern day Christian circles unfortunately one of the first questions that gets asked is "how big is your Church?" rather than "what is God doing in your Church?". We have wrongly associated the size of a congregation with the success of a ministry. This focus has seen the size of our Churches become a measuring stick for how Churches compare themselves and who they associate with.

Our Churches should always be places where everyone feels welcome, but our first priority should always be ensuring that the Lord is welcomed. In order to grow our congregations and highlight our success and favour with God though, we may focus on creating an atmosphere where people feel welcome and feel like they will want to join. We endeavour to create a culture that is accepting and to do this we try to create a space that appeals to man. This extends beyond our services and includes the programs and outreaches that we conduct. It includes things such as our children's and youth ministries, our small groups and home groups, our new Christian classes etc. It is something that permeates every aspect of what we do. We seek to create spaces that appeal to individuals.

What we do becomes a numbers game, and we seek to be more and more outlandish in an effort to attract more and more people. Our events and programs become more and more elaborate, but the overwhelming focus is to appeal to the flesh of man. As our programs and events get bigger and bigger the appeal to the flesh also increases. We can seek to justify it as outreach but if the primary focus is not on

Jesus, then the focus is off. It is an approach based on the flesh. We have forgotten the truth that God will build his Church **not** man (Matt 16:18, Acts 2:47).

The flow on problem from this is that once we attract a crowd, we want to keep them. This can mean that we can tend to avoid tackling anything that may cause a reaction. Rather than seeking to mature the flock we baby them and seek to continue to meet their needs so that they do not want to go anywhere else. We seek to create a space where the individuals needs are met. In doing this all that we really do is rob the Holy Spirit of His ability to convict as we seek to make manmade situations of comfort and acceptance rather than letting the Spirit of God flow and have His way. The result of this is immature believers that never grow up to handle the meat of the Word. We raise them to believe that Church should be a place where their needs are met and the result is that if they ever feel that their needs aren't met, they leave.

This approach reveals the same immaturity as that of Cain. When the Lord did not look upon Cain's sacrifice with favour, Cain's needs weren't met and in response Cain reacted and ended up leaving the presence of God. It is the fruit that comes from the seed of immaturity. This same seed is planted when we operate on a basis of meeting people's needs. We keep them in an infantile state where they never have to experience any growing pains on their path to maturity. They never have to mature because we continually baby them in an effort to keep them happy.

As the people of God, we are called to make disciples. Discipleship is a journey of growth in our relationship with the Lord. It involves moving from the milk of the Word to the meat of the Word. It is a journey from being a newborn in Christ to being a fully functioning adult in Christ. If there is no clear maturing in our congregations and no clear path for how this is to occur, then it is another sign that the spirit of Cain may be present.

The spirit of Cain may be present if there is an environment of immaturity within our Church.

IF WE HAVE SELF-PROTECTIVE REACTIONS TO THE SPIRITUAL.

When the inferiority of what Cain did was revealed by the fire of the Lord upon Abel's sacrifice, Cain sought to shut down that which reflected badly upon him. He rose in anger killing his brother and in so doing prevented the same thing from ever happening again.

Our reactions may not be as visibly violent as Cain's but if we have self-protective reactions arise within us when we see the fire of the Lord in our services it indicates that the spirit of Cain may be present. This can be evident if we try to regain control of things if we see the Spirit start to move in our congregation. We resist what the Lord is wanting to do and try to keep things at the status quo of what we want or are comfortable with.

We can also see the manifestation of this spirit when we see the fire of the Lord move in other places. These self-protective reactions surface as competition, dismissiveness and in the most extreme cases negatively talking about another Church. We try to shut them down just like Cain did with Abel.

Rather than being open to what the Lord may be wanting to lead us into and correct us from, we immediately shut down anything that differs from how we have determined that we will approach the Lord. We have determined what our approach will look like and rather than be stirred by the fire of the Lord to change our approach we double down on protecting what is ours. Such was Cain's response and such shows that the spirit of Cain may be present. The flesh always resists the Spirit.

IF THERE IS A LACK OF DIVINE FIRE.

This is possibly the greatest indicator that the spirit of Cain may be present. The fire of the Lord falls on acceptable sacrifice. It comes and anoints the people of God for ministry. It moves with signs and wonders. Prophecy flows, healings occur, and people undeniably encounter the living God. Cain approached the Lord but there was no fire! Abel had fire, but Cain did not!

Sadly, in many of our services today the same situation exists, and the most concerning thing is that we as the people of God have gotten so used to the fire not being there that it has become our norm. The thought of God outpouring as He did on the early Church seems farfetched and beyond our expectations, but it should in fact be the baseline from which we operate. The fire of the Lord should be an ever-growing presence in our services. It should be our normal. The truth of scripture is that we should be operating in a greater way than the early Church. They are not our benchmark but our starting point! Sadly, we do not often see this same fire in operation. We have a lot of encounters where we walk away feeling great about our time with the Lord, but the fire just hasn't been there.

The fire of God always falls on acceptable sacrifice, but it cannot fall on a sacrifice where the flesh is being exalted more than the Lord is. If His discernible, Holy fire is not there and present as it was in the early Church, we must examine our way of approach. A lack of fire indicates that our approach is off just like Cain's was. A lack of divine fire shows that the spirit of Cain may be present.

For the Church to step into what God is calling her to, we need His fire. Can you imagine what Gideon's battle would have looked like without the torches? (Judg 7) The fire was such a divine part of that victory and so too is it with the Church today. To receive His fire though, we have to approach His way. If His fire isn't there, our approach is off, and the spirit of Cain may be present. Able had fire, Cain did not!

Whilst we have presented some thoughts above, this is by no means an extensive list about the effects of the spirit of Cain. The examples provided have been given as I have felt the Lord impress them upon my heart. As a reminder the Way of Cain **is not** the satisfaction of the flesh **at the expense** of the glorification of God, but rather where the satisfaction of the flesh has **a greater focus** than the glorification of God.

Cain still approached the Lord; he just didn't do it according to the Lord's way! Our honest reflection to the above examples should indicate to us whether this influence is present or not in our lives and Churches.

In doing this we need to be able to ask ourselves has the focus of our services become on keeping the multitudes happy? Have we sought to satisfy the flesh of the congregation in the hopes of growing a bigger one? Could the spirit of Cain be present?

In days when so much focus, particularly in the western Church, has become on the size of a Church as a sign of Christian success, we need to be vigilant to the spirit of Cain. It will seek to cause us to look at our congregation's size and in an effort to grow and achieve our desired success it will encourage us to slowly adapt our services to satisfy the flesh of those we want to attract. It will seek to cause us to become houses with a focus on pleasing the flesh of man in our approach to God. The end result will be that we may still be approaching the Lord just as Cain still brought an offering, the predominate focus though, just like Cain, will be on the satisfaction of the flesh.

We need to relevant. We need to be modern. We need to reach the next generation. None of these are bad intentions but they cannot be used as an excuse to leave the way of Abel for the way of Cain. Our approach has ever got to be primarily and unwaveringly rooted in the glorification of God. We need to be aware of the influence that the spirit of Cain seeks to have just as Jude was. The spirit of Cain will seek to introduce the flesh in ever increasing ways into our Churches and seek to stifle the maturation of the saints. The enemy does not need to defeat us, he just needs to inhibit us from walking in the fulness of what we are called to. The spirit of Cain does just this. It inhibits our approach by shifting our focus to self and it robs us of the fire of the Lord.

Reflection

We have gone through quite a bit in this section and provided a lot of food for thought. The following questions are provided as points of consideration for us to go over and reflect upon. As we do this, I would encourage us to take a step back and ask the Lord to remove any individual bias that we may have. Our purpose here is not to raise judgment on any Church or individual, but rather to take the time to honestly reflect and see if any of the influence of the spirit of Cain is evident in the Church today as it was in Jude's day. My encouragement would be not to just read over these questions, but spend some time praying and contemplating them:

- Is there a time limit on our services? If so, why?

- Is there a general time limit or song limit on our worship?

- Is there a general limit on the preaching time?

- What things are given time in our services?

- Why do we play the songs we do? Is any part of it to be relevant and contemporary?

- Do we create an atmosphere for worship by turning down the lights and emphasising stage lights?

- Are the messages that are preached focused on making the congregation feel better?

- When was the last time we felt the conviction of the Holy Spirit through a message?

- Do the songs that are sung determine my level of worship?

- Do I go to Church to give or to get?

- What do I look for in worship?

- What is the focus of our programs, ministries and outreaches?

- Do we have clear paths of discipleship and maturation?

- Am I maturing? Are my friends maturing?

- Are the gifts of the Spirit functioning in our services just like the early Church?

- What is our reaction to the fire of the Lord falling in other places? Are we defensive, passive aggressive or just presume the same thing will happen to us without ever considering that we may need to change?

- Are our services based on routine?

- Is there an openness to the things of the Spirit, or are they shut down quickly?

- Is the fire of the Lord present in our services?

- Is the fire of the Lord present in my life?

Prayer

Lord, we pray that if the spirit of Cain is at all present in our lives or in our Churches would you please speak to us about it. Would you please open our eyes to every hidden area and every blind spot that we may have. Would you please speak to us about those places where we may have unconsciously opposed your Spirit and pursued the satisfaction of the flesh.

Forgive us Lord where we have set aside your way of approach and have instead chosen our own way. We ask Heavenly Father that you would remove all flesh from our approach and help us to approach as Abel did and not as Cain.

We pray Lord that you would birth afresh within us a passion to see the fire of God once again fall in our lives and services and a desire to pursue nothing less than this.

In Jesus name.

Amen

The Error of Balaam

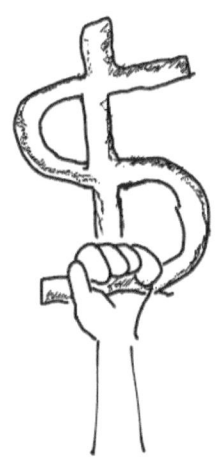

Ran Greedily after the Error of Balaam

> *Woe to them! For they have gone in the way of Cain,* **have run greedily in the error of Balaam for profit***, and perished in the rebellion of Korah. (Jud 1:11) NKJV*

The Individual

Balaam is introduced to us in Numbers 22 where we read that Balak, the king of Moab, sought to hire him to curse the people of Israel who were at the border of Moabite territory. In seeking Balaam's services, Balak sent unto him the elders of Moab and the elders of Midian with the rewards of divination. This would seem to be a payment that was required for Balaam's services. When the elders arrived, they spoke the king's words to Balaam. Rather than just accepting the request and the profits that came from it, Balaam told the elders to lodge for the night while he waited for the Lord to speak to him about the matter. What we read next presents the first conundrum of this account, as we discover that the Lord came and spoke with Balaam during the night. From this account we see that it wasn't just God speaking though, this was a conversation that went back and forth between Balaam and the Lord. We know that Balaam was not a child of

Israel, and we also understand that he was known as a diviner and yet there was clearly a relationship with the Lord that existed. From the inference of scripture this conversation between the Lord and Balaam was not a new thing but an established relationship between the two of them. So, from this initial introduction we see Balaam as a diviner, who received payment to prophecy but also had a relationship with the Lord. Such can bend our mind a little in regard to how the Lord works.

During Balaam's communication with the Lord, the Lord told Balaam not to go with the kings' messengers. The people of Israe were blessed by the Lord and were not to be cursed. The next morning, Balaam went back to the kings' messengers and plainly told them that the Lord had not given him permission to go with them. The messengers then subsequently returned to king Balak and reported all of Balaam's words and his refusal to come at the king's request. King Balak was not satisfied with Balaam's response though and sent unto him princes who were more numerous and more honourable in an attempt to woo Balaam. This time though they did not just go with the diviners' fee but also with the promise that Balaam would be greatly honoured and that the king would do whatever he said. When the messengers arrived and spoke with Balaam, Balaam again had these new messengers lodge for the night while he waited on and sought the Lord. Interestingly though, Balaam did tell them even if Balak would reward him with gold and silver in abundance he could still only do that which the Lord told him. That night the Lord came to him, but this time the message was very succinct and very much directed toward Balaam:

> *And God came to Balaam at night and said to him,* **"If the men come to call you, rise and go with them; but only the word which I speak to you—that you shall do."** *(Num 22:20) NKJV*

In the morning, Balaam saddled his donkey and went with the Balak's messengers. In the next verse though we read that the anger of the Lord was aroused because Balaam went with the men. This response of the Lord can seem contradictory to His words the night before (vs20), but it is actually the actions of Balaam here that we need to focus in on as they give us the further insights into the character of the man. If we look at exactly what the Lord said to Balaam, His words were "**IF** the men come to call thee, rise up and go with them". The Lord did not say no straight out this time, but what He did say was that Balaam could only go **IF** the men came and called him. Balaam's ability to go was conditional. What we read in Numbers though is that in the morning Balaam rose, saddled his donkey and went. We never read that the men came and called him! What we see here is a test upon the heart of Balaam and the result that we see is Balaam being led by the lusts of the flesh rather than the Word of the Lord. The promise of reward and honour caused Balaam to wander into the area of presumption. The Lord had already told Balaam he wasn't to curse the people of Israel, nothing had changed in that regard. This was a test of Balaam's heart and one that Balaam failed. The Lord didn't say no so therefore it must be ok! The men never came though according to the Lord's condition and as such Balaam stepped onto the grounds of disobedience when he rose and left. That is why the Lord's anger was aroused.

It is interesting for us to note that the difference between Balaam's initial obedience and steadfastness to the Lord with his first response compared to his subsequent presumption and disobedient response to the Lord centred around the difference in the magnitude of rewards offered to him. Balaam found it easy to say no when he was only offered the diviners fee. He found it less easy to say no when he was promised riches and honour. The gold and the glory had a corrupting effect on the heart of Balaam. The desire for the rewards and profits of the world caused Balaam to hear that which he wanted to from the Lord.

As Balaam sets out in disobedience to the Word of the Lord, the Lord stood in his way to oppose him. The angel of the Lord literally stood in the path of Balaam to stop his progression down his rebellious path. As Balaam rode along on his donkey with his two servants, the donkey saw the angel of the Lord standing in the way with his sword drawn ready to strike Balaam down. Twice the donkey turned aside from the angel to save Balaam and each time the donkey was struck by Balaam for its seeming disobedience.

On the third occasion the Angel of the Lord stood in a narrow way where the donkey could not turn to the right or to the left. With no other choices available, the donkey laid down. Balaam's anger was immediately aroused at this action of the donkey and Balaam repeatedly struck the donkey with his staff. It was a cruel rage of frustration from Balaam as he beat his donkey in an effort to get it to do what he wanted. As Balaam beat his donkey the Lord opened the mouth of the donkey to be able to speak. The Donkey spoke and asked Balaam a question, "Why have you struck me these three times?" There are two thoughts of interest from this. One the donkey had eyes to see the angel when Balaam didn't. And two, the Lord opened the mouth of a donkey before he opened the eyes of Balaam.

The Donkey spoke before Balaam saw!

Such was the blind rage of Balaam that without thinking and without hesitation he answered the donkey:

> *And Balaam said unto the ass, Because thou hast mocked me: I would there were a sword in mine hand, for now would I kill thee.*
> *(Num 22:29) KJV*

The donkey that Balaam was riding upon was making his journey easier and yet in a state of pure rage Balaam was prepared to make his own journey harder by killing the donkey because he felt that his pride had been attacked. Balaam wasn't content with simply beating the donkey, he wanted to kill it. In Balaam's eyes the donkey had made him look foolish and possibly even embarrassed him in front of his servants and the servants of Balak. Such was Balaam's indignation from this that he was ready to kill his donkey. His pride fuelled anger produced an irrational response. When pride feels threatened it will lash out in irrational and illogical ways, seeking to kill that which it feels has threatened it, even if it means killing something that has been a blessing and even if killing it will make the journey harder. Think of king Saul when David was credited with killing tens of thousands! Saul's pride was ready to see David slain, despite the effect it would have had on his army and their future battles! (1 Sam 18)

What is amazing at this point is that such was the rage of Balaam that he hadn't taken thought that he was engaging in conversation with an animal! What kind of rage must this have been? What does this rage speak to us about Balaam? Rather than checking if his faithful, loyal animal was ok when it started behaving oddly his first response was to kill it for the embarrassment it had caused him. Such reveals a self-interested, egotistical, prideful nature of the man who was focused on his public appearance and the honour that he felt he should be held in. When pride feels attacked it reveals itself as an ugly beast.

The donkey then responded to Balaam's wish to kill it and challenged him by asking, "is this my normal behaviour?" Such a challenge seems to still Balaam as the only response that he could muster was "no". It is as if a sudden realisation came upon Balaam. No this isn't your normal behaviour, and neither is it normal that you are talking. One can almost picture the expression of Balaam change as this realisation hit him. It is then that the Lord opened the eyes of Balaam to see the angel that was standing to oppose him, at which point Balaam immediately falls on his face. The Lord then rebuked Balaam for this treatment of the donkey and informed him that the donkey had actually saved his life. The Lord told Ballam that He had stood to oppose him because his way was perverse and if the donkey hadn't turned aside Balaam would have died but the donkey would have lived. Balaam then repented and the Lord gave him permission to continue on his journey, but He warned him that he must only speak that which the Lord would tell him to. Such was a check from the Lord for Balaam. It was a recentering from the focus of glory and honour to again being obedient to the Word of the Lord. Such seemed to create a lasting sombreness in Balaam as when he came before Balak we read.

> *Then Balak said to Balaam, "Did I not earnestly send to you, calling for you? Why did you not come to me? Am I not able to honor you?" And Balaam said to Balak, "Look, I have come to you!* **Now, have I any power at all to say anything? The word that God puts in my mouth, that I must speak.***" (Num 22:37-38) NKJV*

Whether he liked it or not, Balaam knew he could not wander into presumption. He had to be obedient unto the Word of the Lord.

As we continue in Numbers, we read of three prophetic blessings that Balaam spoke over the nation of Israel, contrary to king Balak's wishes for Israel to be cursed. In each case we read that the Lord met with Balaam, or the spirit of God came upon him. Again, we see that this was an individual who had a relationship with the Lord! By all accounts this man was a prophet of God! What complicates our understanding of Balaam further is what we read with Balaam's third prophecy. Before each time that Balaam prophesied, he had altars and sacrifices prepared in order to seek the Lord. Each time seven altars were built, and seven bulls and rams were prepared for him to offer on each altar. He approached by way of sacrifice, but in Numbers 24:1 as Balaam prepared to approach the Lord a third time, we are given further details of just how he approached:

> *And when Balaam saw that it pleased the LORD to bless Israel,* **he went not, as at other times, to seek for enchantments**, *but he set his face toward the wilderness.*
> *(Num 24:1)*

Balaam had already had seven altars built and had offered seven bulls and seven rams on them when we come to this verse. The clear implication from this is that Balaam in his first two prophesies not only approached by the route of sacrifice but also through enchantments. Balaam would sacrifice and then he would use enchantments in seeking the Lord. In his third prophesy though he saw that enchantments weren't necessary as it pleased the Lord to bless Israel. What we see here is a completely flawed approach unto the Lord and yet the Lord still met with Balaam. Such seems so paradoxical to the modern Christian mind, that one could seem to have such a flawed approach with enchantments and sorcery and yet the Lord spoke to him. Such is also a scary thought for modern believers that the Lord may still meet with us even if our approach is flawed!

What is worthy to note though is that with Balaam's first two prophecies we are told that the Lord met with him. With this third prophecy though where Balaam did not use enchantments the Lord did not just met with him, but the Word says that the Spirit of God came upon him. It would seem to point to a deeper encounter as Balaam's approach aligned with the truth.

After the third utterance of Balaam and the continued blessing of Israel, the anger of Balak was stirred and he told Balaam that the Lord had prevented him from being honoured. Balaam responded and said:

> *So Balaam said to Balak, "Did I not also speak to your messengers whom you sent to me, saying, 'If Balak were to give me his house full of silver and gold, I could not go beyond the word of the LORD, to do good or bad of my own will. What the LORD says, that I must speak'? (Num 24:12-13) NKJV*

Balaam then spoke one final prophetic word regarding the nation of Israel before returning unto his place.

From our look at Numbers 22 -24 we see that Balaam is quite a complicated individual:

- He was not a member of the nation of Israel and yet he was a prophet of the Lord.
- He had a flawed approach unto the Lord and yet the Lord still met with him.
- He was known as a diviner, yet he was clearly prophetic.
- His ministry was based upon payment of the diviner's fee.
- He desired honour and had a problem with pride.
- His pride caused anger, rage, irrational and illogical responses.
- He was obedient yet wandered in presumption.
- He denied the riches of the world with his words but was drawn to them with his actions.

The biggest realisation I had from this look at Balaam was that Balaam was a prophet of the Lord. I had always seen Balaam as a "bad guy", an enemy of Israel, an almost false prophet and whilst there is truth to that, scripture clearly shows that he was an individual who not only had a relationship with the Lord, but spoke with the Lord, received visions from the Lord, spoke prophetic blessings and also prophesied over the future of Israel and about the Messiah. Balaam was a prophet! Now there are undeniably areas of his life and ministry that are askew, but scripture clearly reveals to us that this was an individual who had frequent encounters with the Lord and was one who spoke the words of the Lord out.

We see with Balaam someone who is walking in relationship with the Lord, who is in a prophetic office and is recognised as such, but there are clear flaws in their approach. We very much see with Balaam similar truths to that which we discovered with Cain. These are both individuals who are in relationship with the Lord. In modern terms we would call them Christians or believers. And yet from what we see from scripture is that their paths are amiss. And for me that is the scary part. These are not back slidden, rebellious individuals who have walked away from the Lord. These are individuals who are in relationship with God and conversing with Him!

Having gained an understanding that Balaam was actually a prophet of the Lord, the application of Balaam takes on a whole new meaning.

The Path

> Ran *Greedily after* **the error of Balaam for reward** *(Jud 1:11) KJV*

> *Have run greedily in* **the error of Balaam for profit.** *(Jud 1:11) NKJV*

The question for us to now consider is what is the error of Balaam? Is this referring to the error Balaam made in arising to go to Balak where the Lord stood to oppose him? Whilst that was a part of Balaam's error, it was not the fulness of the error of Balaam. Balaam's actions there reveal to us the seed that would ultimately be the cause of the error of Balaam. We see there that Balaam lusted after the rewards offered to him, but upon the

Lord's correction Balaam remained obedient and did not pronounce a curse upon the nation of Israel. Whilst the desire for reward was there, it had not yet fully manifested itself as the error of Balaam. In order to see the fulness of Balaam's error we need to dive a little further into scripture.

In Numbers 31:8, in talking of the conquests of the people of Israel we read:

> *They killed the kings of Midian with the rest of those who were killed—Evi, Rekem, Zur, Hur, and Reba, the five kings of Midian.* **Balaam the son of Beor they also killed with the sword.** *(Num 31:8) NKJV*

As we read this verse, we may well ask why would Israel slay Balaam and why would the Lord want that fact recorded specifically in scripture? Was not Balaam a follower of God? Was he not a prophet of the Lord? Did he not prophesy blessing after blessing upon the nation of Israel?

The answer as to why Balaam was slain by Israel and why the Lord has this fact recorded in scripture is provided a little further along in Numbers 31:16.

> *Behold, these caused the children of Israel,* **through the counsel of Balaam, to commit trespass against the LORD in the matter of Peor**, *and there was a plague among the congregation of the LORD. (Num 31:16) KJV*

We are told here that the people of Midian through the counsel of Balaam caused the people of Israel to sin against the Lord. In other words, on the advice of Balaam the people of Moab and Midian caused the people of Israel to trespass against the Lord. To fully understand the connotations of this we first need to understand what is meant by the matter of Peor for this is where the trespass occurred. This is detailed for us in Numbers 25 where we read that the people of Israel began to commit sin with the women of Moab.

> *Now Israel remained in Acacia Grove, and the people began to commit harlotry with the women of Moab. They invited the people*

> *to the sacrifices of their gods, and the people ate and bowed down to their gods.* **So Israel was joined to Baal of Peor,** *and the anger of the LORD was aroused against Israel. (Num 25:1-3) NKJV*

For context Balaam and Balak part ways at the end of Numbers 24 with Balaam unable to curse the people of Israel at Balak's request. Then in Numbers 25 we read that the Israel committed sin with daughters of Moab, those who king Balak ruled over. The men of Israel committed sin with the women of Moab and Midian and the people of Moab then called Israel to join them in sacrificing unto their gods. Israel responded to this invitation and joined themselves to Baal of Peor, forsaking the one true living God. This is the matter of **PEOR**. Israel, the chosen nation, set apart for the Lord, willingly joined themselves to one of the nations who knew not the Lord. They were enticed and corrupted themselves. They willingly choose to step away from the commandments of the Lord, indulge in the lusts of the flesh and worship foreign gods as they were encouraged by this corrupting influence. It was a destructive corrupting influence that drew the people of God off the narrow road and onto the broad way that leads to destruction. In response to the actions of the Israelites, the judgement of the Lord broke out upon the nation and twenty-four thousand Israelites died in a plague of the Lord. The holiness of the Lord burned against their blatant sin. This was a matter that Israel would long remember.

In the Numbers 31 verse we have quoted above, we read that the Moabites and Midianites (theses terms are used somewhat interchangeably between Numbers 25 and Numbers 31) deliberately came to the Israelites with the goal of getting them to trespass against the Lord through the **COUNSEL** of Balaam. This was not accidental or coincidental. What happened was a deliberate plan on the part of the enemies of Israel. It was a thought-out attack that had been planned to get a desired result. It was not an attack of physical violence or war, but a spiritual attack of compromise that sought to have a corrupting influence upon the people of God. It came as a trojan horse and had the exact same effect. It was the world seeking to introduce leaven into the people of God.

The book of Revelation expands on this event further where in speaking to the Church at Pergamos Jesus stated:

> *But I have a few things against you, because you have there those who hold the doctrine of Balaam,* **who taught Balak** *to put a stumbling block before the children of Israel, to eat things sacrificed to idols, and to commit sexual immorality. (Rev 2:14)*
> *NKJV*

Balaam did not just counsel Israels enemies, he **TAUGHT** them! Balaam taught Balak to cast a stumbling block before the children of Israel by having them eat food sacrificed unto idols and by committing fornication with the women of Moab. Balaam was not permitted by the Lord to pronounce a curse upon the nation of Israel and receive Balak's rewards, but Balaam knew how the people of Israel could bring a curse upon themselves! The initial seed of a lust for wealth and honour we saw evidenced in Balaam blossoms into full maturity here. The lure of riches and honour proved too much for Balaam. Whilst Balaam knew he could not curse the people of God he also knew that he could advise Balak on how the people of God could bring a curse upon themselves. That is what he did. Through his advice and counsel to Balak, Balaam ensured that not only would the people of Israel remove themselves from being under the blessing of obedience and onto the grounds of disobedience, but that he would receive the promised rewards of riches and honour because of this.

With Balaam we see the lust and pursuit of wealth and honour at the expense of the advancement of the people of God. Balaam was willing for the people of God to wander from the path of obedience for sake of his own personal benefit. It is the corrupted desire for honour and riches that means an individual, even a prophet of the Lord, can be lured by what blesses them with little regard for how the people of God will be affected. This is the error of Balaam.

We need to remember that Balaam was a prophet of the Lord! He was one who had close personal encounters with the Lord and yet his concern for himself outweighed his care for the people of God. Like with Cain, we see a complete lack of any shepherding heart and a complete focus on self.

Balaam's focus was on what blessed him and the security that he got from those things.

> *Which* **have forsaken the right way, and are gone astray, following the way of Balaam** *the son of Bosor,* **who loved the wages of unrighteousness;** *(2Pe 2:15)*
> KJV

Balaam had wandered from the right way and gone astray. He was a prophet of God and yet the wages of unrighteousness lured him away. The error of Balaam is rooted in money and pride. Self is never satisfied with what it currently has in either of these departments and continually lusts for more. It is never content with what it has been blessed with and will continually seek more and more with no regard for the impacts on those around it. It seeks to satisfy its own appetite even if it means hindering the advancement of the people of God. It will start out as a seed, but if it is not dealt with it will fully mature into the error of Balaam.

With our knowledge of Balaam and his relationship with the Lord, one has to wonder how was he ever able to justify his actions against the people of Israel? How could Balaam who knew that the Lord was for the people of Israel justify in his mind that it would be ok for him to teach Balak how to make the people of Israel stumble in their relationship with the Lord? I would suggest that within Balaam there was possibly a level of religiousness. If we look at his approach unto the Lord, each time Balaam did the exact same thing with erecting altars and offering sacrifice, down to the very number of sacrifices he offered. His approach was rooted in routine. A religious spirit will always seek to define rules for how things are to be done and followed. This was the same spirit at work in the Pharisees and Sadducees in Jesus day with their love for rules and regulations. It was this same spirit that let them pay Judas to betray Jesus and yet seemingly remain clean themselves. Technically they had done nothing wrong! In the same sense technically Balaam had not done anything wrong. He had not cursed Israel and had remained obedient unto the word of the Lord. Technically! But what we know from scripture is that the Lord looks at the heart and Balaam's heart was found wanting.

In the error of Balaam we see presumption, irrational and illogical pride and anger, religiousness, and a focus on the gold and the glory which ultimately manifested in a satisfaction of self at the expense of the advancement of the people of God. It is truly a tragic tale.

In Balaam we truly see the truth of Matt 13:

> *He also that received seed among the thorns is he that heareth the word; and* **the care of this world, and the deceitfulness of riches**, *choke the word, and he becometh unfruitful.* *(Mat 13:22) KJV*

Notice it says that the cares of the world and the deceitfulness of riches choke the word so that the individual **BECOMES UNFRUITFUL.** It doesn't say that they are unfruitful, but that they will become unfruitful. It is a process of decline. The thorns are weeds that grow gradually choke the fruitful tree. It is a process of suffocation where life is slowly taking away to the point where the tree can no longer bear fruit. It had once been fruitful, but through the choking of the world and riches it becomes less and less fruitful until it reaches the point of bareness. It is a process of fruitful decline. Balaam was one who undeniably heard the word of the Lord, but the cares of the world (the desire for the honour of man) and the deceitfulness of riches truly choked his life, and he became unfruitful. The lusts of flesh caused compromise in Balaam.

Balaam chased reward, but we cannot serve both God and money. Unfortunately for Balaam his actions showed where his heart truly lay and greater was his love for wealth and honour than it was for the Lord. Balaam was a man of compromise, and this same compromise was introduced to the Church in the wilderness through his advice. The world can have no place in us individually or corporately. The Lord must continually be on throne of our lives. Then and only then can we truly walk according to His ways.

The Action

Ran greedily *after the error of Balaam for reward (Jud 1:11)*
KJV

With Cain we read that the individuals had gone in the way of Cain. It spoke of a choice of path. With the path of Balaam we see an increase in momentum. The Greek word for 'ran greedily' means to "pour forth, to shed forth, to bestow or distribute largely". Its connotations are around the momentum that comes when something is poured out. There is motion to it. It is a gaining of speed like waters breaking forth from a dam. That is what it is with the error of Balaam. It is an increase in momentum from that of Cain. It is a change of language from having chosen a path to that of eager pursuit. It is going from a walk to a run. It speaks of an effort and a motion to get to a desired target.

Balaam didn't just look for reward, he pursued and chased after it. He did everything he could to get it. And it is the same with the individuals that Jude is referring to. There is a focus and a pursuit of the individual rewards. For me this presents the image of an individual in a race, but they are pushing, tripping and blatantly hindering the other competitors to get the goal. It is an all-consuming pursuit of reward with no regard for how anyone else is affected.

What starts with Cain gains momentum with Balaam.

The spirit of Balaam

We now turn our attention to consider the spirit of Balaam and what could be some indications that it could be in operation in our lives and Churches. We will again here seek to apply the lessons we have learnt from Balaam to our modern-day environment in an effort to try and discern if that spirit is present.

At the expense of repetition, I would again say that this is written as a means of introspection not with a focus on any individual or Church and I would encourage you again to take a moment to stop and pray for an open and discerning heart before moving forward here. Our goal is to understand the words of Jude's warning and understand how these spirits work against the modern Church and the believers within it.

The Spirit of Balaam may be present:

IF THERE IS A FOCUS ON THE PURSUIT OF MONEY.

With Balaam, we see a clear pursuit of money. His ministry was based on money, and he pursued the riches that Balak offered unto him. Whilst his words may have been that he could not be enticed by riches, his actions clearly show us what his heart was focused on.

It was the Lord Jesus who said:

> *"No one can serve two masters; for either he will hate the one and love the other, or else he will be loyal to the one and despise the other. You cannot serve God and mammon. (Mat 6:24) NKJV*

What we can decipher from this statement of Jesus is that mammon opposes the position of God in our lives. It seeks to be number one in the heart and mind of man and replace God on the throne of our lives. It seeks mastery over mankind. Balaam so clearly illustrates this truth. If he had completely submitted to God as his master, then the rewards of Balak would have been inconsequential to him and he would have despised them just like Elisha did with the rewards offered to him by Naaman (2 Kings 5). Balaam though was under the mastery of mammon, and it was mammon which he pursued. He followed God but he served mammon. His actions and outcome are a clear example of the words of Jesus.

Just like Balaam, a focus on mammon isn't always revealed by words. Our mouth may speak the right things, but it is our heart and our actions that truly reveal who has mastery of our heart. If we are able to take a Holy Spirit led honest and open introspective reflection on our actions, individually and corporately, it will reveal to us whether mammon is an issue. Why have we made certain decisions? Why did we choose certain courses of action? What was leading our thought processes?

The real problem is that the pursuit of mammon denies the Lord as Jehovah Jireh. It says that money is the answer to our needs and so the answer lies in pursuing and gaining more of it. It becomes our source of provision and suddenly the Lord is standing on the sidelines as we bypass Him and chase the dollar. We are not talking about having a focus on faithful stewardship with our finances here, for that is something we all must do, but rather a lust and pursuit for riches that is never satisfied. What we have is never enough and we are always looking for opportunities to get more for our own benefit.

The spirit of Balaam may be present if there is a focus on money.

IF THERE IS A FEE FOR SERVICE MENTALITY.

Notice that when king Balak initially sent for Balaam he sent the "Diviner's Fee". As we read about Balaam, we discovered that he was a prophet of the Lord who spoke with God and heard from Him. Balaam had a prophetic gift, but he did not operate as other Old Testament prophets. Balaam operated on a fee for service mentality. The use of his gift was based on what he would receive. One has to ask, if Balak had not sent the diviners fee would Balaam had even taken the night to pray about whether he should go with the messengers, or would he just have sent the messengers away? Given what we know about Balaam it would be safe to assume that he well might have sent them away. With Balaam we see the monetisation of a ministry, where the material wealth of an individual or Church determines whether or not they receive ministry.

Any ministry should be based completely and solely on what the command of the Lord is and never based on a fee mentality. Balaam's ministry sees only those who can afford it receive it. It is an elitist approach that overlooks the poor and the widow and looks to minister to only those of a certain standing. It is an approach completely opposite to that of the Lord Jesus.

If in any of our thinking Church size, location or what they can afford plays a part in whether or not they are ministered to, then it indicates that the spirit of Balaam may be present. Our primary motivating factor should always be based on what does the Lord want. Nothing else should ever come into the equation, otherwise we risk following the same path as Balaam. Where would the Church today be if the early apostles had operated on this premise? It would not have gotten very far as when the Church was birthed there were not many paying customers so to speak. The apostles very much operated off the command of freely you have received, freely give (Matt 10:8). This same sentiment should echo through all that we as the Church do today as well.

IF THERE IS A DESIRE FOR GREATER RECOGNITION.

The difference between the first approach of Balak to Balaam and the second was the amount of reward and also the promise of honour and recognition. It was the promise of honour and recognition that drew on the pride of Balaam. Balaam and his ministry were clearly already recognised and known, that is why king Balak sent for him. Yet this was not enough for Balaam, he desired greater recognition and honour. It was a pursuit based in pride.

The need for recognition speaks to a lack of contentment. It is an indicator that we are not satisfied with the level of honour, respect and even fame that we think we are deserving of. This goes beyond us being faithful with the gifts that God has given to us and involves us looking to only "serve" in areas where those giftings are recognised in a greater way. The problem with this though is that self and pride are never satisfied with the recognition they get. They are always wanting and demanding more and as such will always look for further opportunities where that need for recognition can be satisfied. This was the issue with Balaam. He was not satisfied with the recognition he had; he desired more and once that carrot was waved in front of him, he pursued it until he got what he desired.

This desire can extend beyond a personnel level and can include the motivation for our Church ministries and outreaches. Are we focused on giving without our left hand knowing what our right hand is doing or are the activities we undertake so stamped with our Churches branding that there is no mistaking who is undertaking things? What is the main motivation? Is it possibly for recognition? A good indicator can be that if with each succeeding activity we undertake we seek to get the name of "our" Church out there more. Whether individually or corporately the motivation behind everything we do should be for **JESUS** to be recognised not us. Anytime we take any recognition for ourselves or our ministry we diminish that which rightly belongs to Him.

> *But he that is greatest among you shall be your servant. And whosoever shall exalt himself shall be abased; and he that shall humble himself shall be exalted. (Mat 23:11-12) KJV*

To that extent it should not matter if the ministry or event we conduct sees new converts end up attending another Church! Often, we can get so focused on the benefits of reaping for our barn that we miss the Kingdom principle. The importance lays not in whether our barn grows, but that the Kingdom barn grows. The Apostle Paul touches on this in the book of Corinthians:

> *Who then is Paul, and who is Apollos, but ministers through whom you believed, as the Lord gave to each one? I planted, Apollos watered, but God gave the increase. So then neither he who plants is anything, nor he who waters, but God who gives the increase. Now he who plants and he who waters are one, and each one will receive his own reward according to his own labor. For we are God's fellow workers; you are God's field, you are God's building. (1Co 3:5-9) NKJV*

He that plants and he that waters are one. They are both just servants of God playing their part in Kingdom advancement. It is God who gives the increase and neither individual nor Church is lessened by the work of the other. God is Kingdom focused! He does not look at Church size. His focus is on whether we are being faithful in the part we are called to play, whether that is planting or whether that is watering.

If our focus is on Kingdom advancement, then the success of another Church will not affect us. If though our focus is on greater recognition, we may feel some pangs when others reap the fruit of our sowing.

IF WE HAVE IRRATIONAL AND ILLOGICAL RESPONSES.

We saw with Balaam that when his pride falsely felt that it had been attacked, his anger and rage reached such a point that he started arguing with a donkey about his desire to kill it. He was then rebuked by the donkey for his actions and words before he even had the presence of mind to realise what was happening. What kind of rage must this have been for Balaam to not even blink at the fact that the donkey was talking, and he was conversing with it? The donkey had been loyal, the donkey had been faithful, the donkey had served him for years. The donkey was making Balaam's life and journey easier and whilst he didn't realise it the donkey was looking out for Balaam and protecting him from what he couldn't yet see. Balaam though only wrongly perceived that he was being made to look foolish and because of this he was prepared to kill the donkey. Had the Lord not intervened what would Balaam have done here?

There was pride in Balaam and his reaction came from the fact that he felt he was being disrespected publicly. It was pride that prevented Balaam from looking beyond himself to check on the donkey who was acting out of character and it was this same pride that produced a response that made no sense. Balaam was ready to kill the ministry of the donkey because he felt his position, place and person had been disrespected. Balaam felt he was being mocked and as such sought to repay the donkey for this. Pride will always seek retribution; wisdom though seeks understanding!

In light of this, some questions for us to consider are: How do I respond when people seemingly disrespect me, my office or my ministry? Do my walls go up? Do I seek to distance the individual?

We can take this a step further and ask how does our Church handle individuals who would seem to be disrespectful or not showing the proper honour? Are they shut down, shut off, excluded or demoted? What has been the reason for ceasing ministries or changing teams and leaders?

The Holy Spirit does give us a spirit discernment and at times that will mean distancing some relationships, but the Holy Spirit will always work in love. What we are looking at here though is over-the-top responses that are spurned from anger and seek the detriment of the individual through any means possible. Wounded pride responds like a wounded animal. It kicks and thrashes with little care or thought as to the consequences. It seeks to inflict on an individual what which it has felt. This is what happened with Balaam, he was prepared to make his own journey much harder than it needed to be for the sake of getting retribution for dented pride. It is short term thinking based on the individual who has been wounded feeling better about themselves by taking their anger out on whom they believe is the culprit. This is why Balaam wanted to attack his donkey. He wanted to work his rage out and channel it at that which he thought had disrespected him. "You've done this to me therefore I'll do this to you!"

A way to identify this spirit is to reflect on the reasons why past major decision in our lives and Churches have been made.

- Have they been reactionary or have they been thought out and prayed over?

- Have they been made by one person or have two or three been involved in this process?

- In reflection have they been both rational and logical decisions or irrational and illogical?

- Has pride played any part in the decision being made?

- Can we see any evidence of payback in the decisions that have been made?

Honest answers to these questions will provide us with insights into whether the spirit of Balaam may be present. It takes a humble heart to see and recognise pride and that can only come when we are prepared to admit that we may have been wrong. When we humble ourselves before the Lord and ask for His input into our actions, we allow His Spirit to speak to our hearts and reveal anything that we may be blinded to.

IF WE USE RELIGIOUS JUSTIFICATION FOR OUR ACTIONS.

As we noted in our look at Balaam, Balaam was possibly able to justify his actions to himself as he technically did not break the word of the Lord. At no stage did he ever verbally pronounce a curse upon the nation of Israel. His justification was based upon a religious technicality, much like the Pharisees and Sadducees of Jesus day.

Religious justification is something that can be used in spite of the fact that we know we are neglecting the truths of God and His Word. An example of how this can manifest in our days is along the lines of statements that sound like "we don't focus on that as we want to show people God's love and not make them feel judged". Whilst seemingly innocent and even well meaning, what we are in fact saying is that we are deliberately avoiding certain topics, but our reason is to show God's love. It is the same religious justification that Balaam used. We are technically not doing anything wrong, we are preaching part of the gospel, but we are deliberately circumventing the truth of what God has called us to do. Balaam tried to do the same. God is not mocked though, and He sees the heart beyond the motive. He is not a God of technicalities!

If we try to justify deliberately neglecting the fulness of the gospel then it may be an indicator that the spirit of Balaam is present.

IF THERE IS A GREATER FOCUS ON PERSONNEL OR CORPORATE ADVANCEMENT RATHER THAN KINGDOM ADVANCEMENT.

This is possibly one of the biggest effects that we see from the spirit of Balaam. It is seen when our individual advancement or the Churches advancement supersedes that of the Kingdom's advancement.

On a personnel level we may feel that this is an easier thing to identify. That is true when we look at it from the point of view of an individual pursuing worldly glory rather than Kingdom glory. But what if we were to look at it from a 'spiritual' point of view. At the heart of the spirit of Balaam is the promotion of self with no regards for the effects to the people of God. In modern terms this could be an individual seeking to build and promote their own ministry. This is not always the case, but where there is a focus on networking, building relationships, building a profile and seeking pulpits and ministry opportunities with the sole focus to build one's own ministry then it could indicate that the spirit of Balaam is present. After all, that is what Balaam was after, the promotion and honour of his name. He wrongly associated the success of the world with Godly success. The key to identifying whether we are motivated like this is when it becomes more about us than about what will advance the Kingdom. Indicators could be:

- If we were to ever strategically think about ministry opportunities.
- If we were to look at some opportunities as beneath our abilities or callings.
- If we seek to monopolise a pulpit at every opportunity.
- If we look for opportunities to be on the microphone.
- If we control a pulpit so no threats to our ministry can arise.
- If we publicly speak badly of other ministries similar to ours.

- If throughout our messages we have an exaggerated focus on self.

- If we see other ministries as threats rather than co-labourers.

- If we operate with a strong sense of control to ensure we remain on top.

Such thoughts are humbling to think about, but it is the underlying motivation that reveals whether there is an issue or not and this is only something that can truly be discovered by taking the time to seek the Lord and truly introspect on our actions. What I would say is that pride will quickly dismiss the above-mentioned thoughts, but a heart that is focused on Kingdom advancement will be humble enough to seek the Lord about them because at the end of the day a heart that is truly focused on Kingdom advancement wants to make sure that they do not do anything to impede it.

Having looked at an individual level, the question now becomes what does this look like from a corporate or Church point of view? From a corporate sense this looks like wanting to maintain and build a socially acceptable image. It is when the Church image becomes the main objective. It is when a Church is more focused on keeping a crowd than seeing the congregation advance. As any Church grows and attracts new people, its popularity grows, its name grows, its finances grow, and its reach grows. What has started off well suddenly becomes focused on protecting and maintaining what has been built. The focus of Kingdom advancement can shift to maintaining what has been built. As a means to keep the stature and opulence that comes from a larger congregation and the subsequent standing in Christian circles, the temptation can be to try and keep the flock happy. Our focus can shift to keeping the sheep happy rather than seeing the sheep grow and develop. In other words, we can start to avoid messages and topics that would possibly offend some people and instead turn to a more socially acceptable gospel. Rather than raising disciples, we seek to make Church a place that is fun and exciting, where individuals come and walk away feeling good about themselves. All this does though is show that there is a focus of the advancement of the Church at the expense of advancement of the Kingdom in the hearts and lives of believers.

Balaam's focus was on what blessed him and his ministry rather than what saw the Kingdom of God advance. Balaam was indifferent to the effects on the people of God so long as he was blessed. Whilst seemingly harsh, this same spirit seeks to be alive and operating in many Churches today as both Jude and Jesus warn us about (Jude 1:11, Rev 2:14). It is birthed through success and operates under a banner of love and tolerance. What we forget though is that love does not operate in isolation to truth and truth should always be spoken in love. The two work together and one is never at the expense at the other. We are called to love the world, but we are also called to preach the whole truth of the Gospel in love. Our Churches should be houses of truth and love with a focus on the advancement of the Kingdom even if that means risking offending some of the congregation. It is better to be a Church on fire than one that is lukewarm! It is better to be faithful in the eyes of God than successful in the eyes of the world. The spirit of Balaam will always seek to induce fear of what we could lose by focusing on Kingdom advancement. The Holy Spirit though will cause us to see what we could gain even if it is with less!

Kingdom advancement should always be the primary motivating factor for everything we do individually and corporately. Any time that personnel advancement or protection outweighs this we need to take the time to seek the Lord as to whether the spirit of Balaam may be present.

IF COMPROMISE IS EVIDENT.

It was upon the advice of Balaam that worldliness was introduced to the people of God and the people of God were introduced to the world. We see in Numbers an intermingling of the two as the people of God compromised their values and succumbed to the influence of the world. They embraced the world and in so doing quickly adopted the worlds ways, values and practices. The people of Israel compromised what they knew was the truth in order to fulfil the lusts of the flesh as they were drawn into the practices of the world. What is scary is how widely and how quickly this was tolerated amongst the Israelites. This was not just one or two, there was a great multitude affected by this. This compromise quickly spread amongst the people of God. One can almost imagine the conversations, "Oh we are allowed to do that?" …. "Yeah, everybody is".

When we come to the book of Revelation, Jesus in speaking to the Church at Pergamos stated:

> *But I have a few things against thee, because thou hast there* **them that hold the doctrine of Balaam,** *who taught Balac to cast a stumblingblock before the children of Israel, to eat things sacrificed unto idols, and to commit fornication. (Rev 2:14)*

What was the counsel of Balaam in the Old Testament finds itself to be the doctrine of Balaam in the New Testament! We need to remember that Jesus was talking to a Church here and He was telling them that He Knew that there were those in their midst who held to the doctrine of Balaam. There were those that would hold that as a Christian you can in fact have a foot in both camps. There was compromise in this early Church and it was not just accepted, but there was doctrine put forth to support this stance. The doctrine put forth by these believers taught that it was ok for the people of God to act like the world and not so rigidly hold to the standards of the Word. The enemy will always seek to compromise the truth of God in the mind of the believer in order to get them to fall away from the truth of the Word. He did it with Eve, he did it through Balaam and we see the same thing with the Church of Pergamos. The spirit of Balaam was prevalent, and it was causing compromise within the body of Christ. Compromise slowly pulls the people of God further and further from the truth and the only way to deal with it is to address it strongly by drawing a line in the sand. This is what Moses did, and it was what Jesus was doing with the Church at Pergamos.

The people of God are called to be light and in us there should be no darkness. There should be a discernible difference between the people of God and the world. Such is not being legalistic, but biblical. Our speech should be different. Our lifestyles should be different. Our actions and conduct should be different. There should be no compromise with the people of God for when we become like the world, we forfeit the ability to show them the life changing power of God! The complete truth of the Word of God should be preached, and disciples should be raised according to it. Compromise only exists in our lives and in our Churches when the truths of God are neglected!

Compromise can occur as a direct result of the previous point we considered. Just as with Balaam personnel advancement saw compromise introduced, so too is it with us and our Churches. The pursuit of personnel advancement with an eye on the gold and the glory will always see compromise introduced individually and corporately. It is compromise that allows us to pursue worldly success, but it is always at the expense of the advancement of the people of God individually and corporately. The desire to be like the world, to chase the things of the world and the success of the world inevitably opens the people of God up to compromise.

When the people of God start to look and act like the people of the world then it can be an indicator that the spirit of Balaam may be present.

IF THERE IS A LACK OF SPIRITUAL ADVANCEMENT OF THE PEOPLE OF GOD.

The people of God should always be advancing spiritually. Our lives should be being continually transformed as we are changed from glory to glory, more and more into the image of Jesus. That is the process of true Christian discipleship, continual growth. The spirit of Balaam seeks to inhibit this though. It seeks to hinder the people of God and cause them to stagnate in their walk. It seeks to introduce teaching and compromise that sees the people of God inhibited in their ability to grow in their spiritual walk.

In each of our lives, individually and corporately, there should be continual growth and change as we spiritually mature in the faith, and this should be demonstrated by the spiritual fruit that our lives produce. There are seasons where growth can look different. At times our roots will be going deeper and at others our branches will be producing a harvest. But at all times growth should be occurring. If this is not happening, then we need to reflect on why this may be the case. It could be related to the spirit of Balaam. It may be that our growth is being inhibited, and we may need to seek the Lord about why?

A lack of spiritual growth and advancement could indicate that the spirit of Balaam is present.

Again, just like with the spirit of Cain, that which has been presented is not an extensive list of how the spirit of Balaam operates, but rather that which the Lord has quickened to my heart as I have thought and prayed over this topic. I myself have felt challenged and repented in more than one area from what has been presented above.

With the spirit of Balaam we see that there may be giftings of the Lord and moves of the Spirit, as there was on Balaam himself, but there is an underlying focus on the attainment of greater wealth and greater honour. It is a spirit that looks for individual advancement, whether that is of an individual or a Church, without regard for the advancement of the people of God. It places money and honour as of greater importance than the spiritual state and development of believers. If it feels challenged it will lash it with over-the-top responses in an attempt of self-protection. It creates a focus on self-image that is prepared to take down anything and anyone that gets in its way. It will religiously justify its actions but ultimately cause compromise to the people of God and see them stagnate in a state of godliness mixed with worldliness. It is a corrupting influence that appeals to the flesh of man but ultimately seeks to cause the people of God to live in disobedience to the truths of the Word.

The saddest things that we see from this account is that this emanated from a prophet of the Lord, and was quickly adopted, accepted and carried out by the people of Israel. How quickly the people of God were corrupted by this influence. As believers and Churches, we need to be ever aware that this doctrine is alive and well and seeking to infiltrate believers and the

Church today just as it was with the Church at Pergamos. The spirit of Balaam may start with an individual, but its ultimate goal is for the people of God. It is a spirit that seeks to rob the people of God from entering into the fulness of the promises of God by inhibiting their walk through the introduction of compromise.

The spirit of Balaam is birthed through pride and the spirit of mammon. As the people of God, we ever need to be aware of these areas and their presence within our lives and Churches as these would seem to be the starting points from which the spirit of Balaam blossoms. We need to learn from the mistakes of Balaam and deal with these areas before they are allowed to mature and multiply.

Reflection

As we again provide some questions for reflection, I would again encourage us to take the time to seek the Lord for His personnel and corporate insights as we read over the list below:

- Do I seek to build my own profile, or do I seek to raise disciples?

- Does our Church seek to build its profile, or does it seek to raise disciples?

- Do I have a kingdom focus or a personnel focus?

- Do I look for strategic partnerships? Does our Church?

- Am I willing to serve in areas where nobody sees?

- Do I yearn for recognition? Is this ever satisfied?

- Am I always looking for the next big opportunity?

- With the outreach and activities that we undertake is our goal to leave a lasting image of Jesus or a lasting image of our brand?

- Would we have a problem if new believers attended another Church after being reached at one of our events?

- Is there evidence of compromise or worldliness in my life? In our Church?

- Do we preach a message of acceptance or one of divine change?

- Are we prepared to have hard chats about matters of worldliness?

- Do we speak the truth in love, or do we focus more on showing love without necessarily considering truth?

- How do I honestly react when I feel I am not given the proper respect?

- Are my responses Spirit lead? Or are they reactionary to prove a point?

- Are ministry decisions based on where the Lord directs us or are they directed by monetary considerations?

- If there was a choice between two ministry opportunities would financial possibilities or potential recognition play a part in the decision?

- Are the financial blessings of God a continual focus in our prayers, our messages, or our life?

- Am I spiritually advancing? Is my Church spiritually advancing?

- Are we seeing the fruits of maturity in our congregation?

- Are we continually going deeper in the things of God?

Prayer

Lord, we pray that you would open our eyes and hearts to any areas where there may be issues relating to finance and pride. Would you open our eyes to see clearly, and would you give us the humility to accept any correction that may be needed. We repent Lord of anywhere we have allowed the spirit of Balaam to operate, we ask for your forgiveness and we ask you to remove any spots of this error from our lives and Churches.

Dear Lord, would you birth within us a pure unwavering desire to see the advancement of the Kingdom and kill all areas within us that would seek that satisfaction of the flesh. Would you help us to live our lives for your glory and not our own.

Holy Spirit, we give you permission to examine our hearts and reveal any areas of compromise that we may be blind to. Would you please speak to us and give us the strength to deal with anything that we need to.

In Jesus name.

Amen.

The Rebellion of Korah

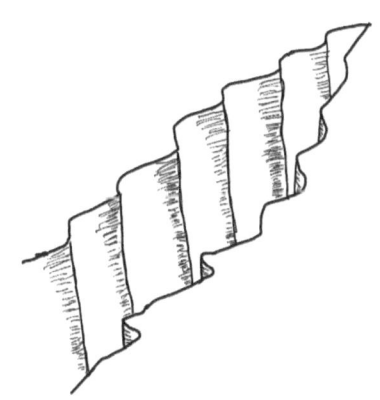

Perished in the Rebellion of Korah

Woe to them! For they have gone in the way of Cain, have run greedily in the error of Balaam for profit, **and perished in the rebellion of Korah.** *(Jud 1:11)* NKJV

The Individual

Our final individual to look at from Jude is Korah. We read of Korah in Numbers 16 and whilst not a lot of information is given about him, we are told that he was of the nation of Israel and a descendant from the tribe of Levi. Korah was of the clan of Kohath and would have served as a priest in the Tabernacle of Moses under the direction of the Aaronic priests. The Lord gave the clan of Kohath the responsibility over the moving and setup of the furniture that resided in the Holy Place and the Most Holy Place during the wilderness wanderings of Israel. This included the responsibility for transporting the Ark of the covenant, the dwelling place and throne of God on the earth. Amongst the clans of Levi, this was an enviable position to have. For Korah though, as we will discover, this was not enough.

We have Korah, a descendant of Israel and a priest of the tribe of Levi who served in the Church in the wilderness.

The Path

> *Woe unto them! for they have .... perished* **in the gainsaying of Core.** *(Jud 1:11) KJV*

> *Woe unto them! For they have .... Perished* **in the rebellion of Korah** *(Jud 1:11) NKJV*

Jude tells us that the individuals he was addressing in the Church had perished in the gainsaying or rebellion of Korah. The word for gainsaying in Greek means dispute or disobedience, opposition or rebellion. In English it carries the thought of contradict or to oppose an individual or group. Korah was an individual who contradicted and opposed Moses and Aaron, and he stood in rebellion and disobedience against the Lord. Korah's path, as we will see, was one of rebellion.

In Numbers 16 we are told that Korah along with Dathan, Abiram and On took some two hundred and fifty men and revolted against the leadership of Moses and Aaron. Whilst Korah is listed as the antagonist in Jude he did not operate alone, he had followers, and he had co-conspirators.

Korah was from the priestly tribe of Levi and as such had a role within the ministry functions of the Tabernacle. Dathan, Abiram and On were the descendants of Rueben. Rueben was the firstborn of Jacob but had forfeited his rights as the firstborn through his indiscretion with his father's concubine.

The chief complaint that these men brought is described for us in Numbers 16:3:

> *They gathered together against Moses and Aaron, and said to them, "You take too much upon yourselves, for all the congregation is holy, every one of them, and the LORD is among them. Why then do you exalt yourselves above the assembly of the LORD?" (Num 16:3) NKJV*

The complaint that these men had was against the position and the place that the Lord had put Moses and Aaron in. It is worth remembering here that scripture records Moses as the humblest man that had walked the earth. He was not a man who was caught up in titles or authority and yet that was the very charge brought against him and Aaron! Such goes to show the heart of the men bringing the accusation. The truth was that they wanted to be the rulers and leaders over Israel. It is interesting to note that one of the translations for Korah is bald, i.e. no covering of hair on the head. It is no coincidence that it was Godly covering that Korah rebelled against. He didn't want to operate under covering; he wanted to be free of it!

In response to this rebellious attack, we read that Moses fell upon his face before then responding to Korah and his followers. It would seem from what transpires next that the two hundred and fifty individuals with Korah were actually also sons of Levi, fellow servants in the priestly class. This was not a stand against corrupt leadership, this was a coup, a grasp for power of the priesthood fuelled by the sons of Rueben.

Moses told Korah and his followers that the next morning they should all come with a censor filled with incense and fire. They would stand with their censors and Aaron would stand with his and the Lord would show whom He had deemed as holy. Incense was something that was offered by the Aaronic priests at the Golden Altar of incense. The Lord had already commanded and ordained this. This test was simply a confirmation that only the ones whom the Lord deemed holy could offer incense unto Him.

Moses then challenged Korah and his followers as to their actual motives:

> *Is it a small thing to you that the God of Israel has separated you from the congregation of Israel, to bring you near to Himself, to do the work of the tabernacle of the LORD, and to stand before the congregation to serve them; and that He has brought you near to Himself, you and all your brethren, the sons of Levi, with you?* **And are you seeking the priesthood also?** *Therefore you and all your company are gathered together against the*

> *LORD. And what is Aaron that you complain against him?"*
> *(Num 16:9-11)*

Moses addressed the heart of the issue. It was not about Moses and Aaron's leadership but over the fact that Korah and his followers desired the priesthood. They were not satisfied with the offices that they had been given as priests who served in the Tabernacle, they wanted the Aaronic priesthood too and the prestige that came with it. This was a jostle for position.

Moses then went on to inform them that whilst in the natural they might be standing against him and Aaron, what they were in fact doing was standing against the Lord's anointed. They had raised their hands against the anointed of the Lord and sought positions that were not theirs to have. They weren't rebelling against Moses and Aaron but against the Lord in their actions. Their challenge was actually about the people whom **THE LORD** had placed over them.

The next day as Korah and his followers gathered at the door of the Tabernacle of Moses with their censors and fire, standing opposite Aaron who stood there alone with his, we are told that Korah also gathered all the congregation against Moses and Aaron. Such was the arrogance and pride of Korah that he sought to make a public display over what he wrongly presumed would be his appointment to office.

As the congregation gathered, the glory of the Lord appeared to all the congregation and the Lord told Moses and Aaron to separate themselves from the congregation, for the He was going to consume the congregation. Such speaks to the magnitude of this rebellion, its infiltration and how God viewed it, that He was going to consume the whole congregation.

Moses and Aaron immediately fell on their faces in intercession for the people of Israel and asked the Lord to only judge the men who had sinned. The same men who are accused of ruling over the people and acting like princes, were on their faces interceding for the lives of the congregation!

The Judgement of the Lord then came against those who had rebelled. The ground opened up and swallowed the tents of Dathan, Abiram and Korah, something that had never been seen before. Fire then came out from the presence of the Lord and consumed the two hundred and fifty men who stood at the door of the Tabernacle with their censors full of incense and fire. The only thing left from this purging fire of the Lord was the censors that the men offered. These were taken by Eleazer the priest and at the command of the Lord were made into a covering for the Brazen Altar that would act as a permanent reminder to the nation of the rebellion of Korah.

Korah was one that rebelled against the leadership of Moses and Aaron and stood in opposition to their God given authority. Korah was a priest of the Lord and yet was unsatisfied with his position. He sought more and the only way to get that was to topple the leadership of the day. As such he plotted and planned on how he could do this. His rebellion was not something that just occurred. It was something that occurred over time as he gathered more followers in an effort to strengthen his challenge. Ultimately though, Korah's challenge was not against Moses or Aaron but against the Lord and as such Korah came under His judgment. Korah, a descendant of Israel and priest of the tribe of Levi, died in disobedience and rebellion to the Lord.

The Action

> *Woe unto them! for they have .... **perished** in the rebellion of Korah. (Jud 1:11) NKJV*

Jude tells us that the individuals he was addressing had gone in the way of Cain, had ran after the error of Balaam but here we are told they perish in the rebellion of Korah. There is a finality to this action.

The Greek word for perish means to destroy fully and it is translated as destroy, die, lose, mar, perish. Korah perished for his rebellion. In applying this I do not believe that Jude is talking about natural death in this verse but rather spiritual death. These individuals had progressed down a path that ultimately saw them spiritually die. That which had once been in them no longer existed. It is an especially horrendous thought when we remember that Jude here was writing to members of a Church. They were in the Church, but God was not in them. They had an appearance of spirituality, but the reality was that within them there was no flame or fire but, as with Korah and his followers, simply ashes of what had once been.

The spirit of Korah

In this section we will turn our attention to consider the spirit of Korah and what could be some indications that it could be in operation in our lives and Churches. As we do this, we will again seek to apply the lessons we have learnt from Korah to our modern-day environment in an effort to try and discern if the spirit of Korah could be present.

Before we do that, my encouragement would be to please take a moment to stop and pray for an open and discerning heart before moving forward here. It is on open, honest and humble heart that keeps us in a position where the Holy Spirit can continue to grow and mature us through His truth.

The spirit of Korah may be present:

IF THERE IS A DISSATISFACTION WITH GOD GIVEN POSITION.

Korah was of the priestly tribe of Levi and, as we discovered, was from the clan of Kohath. His responsibilities included looking after the most holy articles of furniture within the Tabernacle of Moses. He quite possibly could have been one of the priests who bore the Ark of the Lord upon their shoulders. Within this role though, he served under the direction of the Aaronic Priesthood.

Korah had a prominent position, but it wasn't the most prominent and Korah was clearly dissatisfied with where he found himself. One has to wonder what were the inner talking's of Korah, Dathan and Abiram? Was Korah to replace Aaron and Dathan and Abiram to replace Moses? I would suggest that this was most likely the case. Whenever there is a rebellion there is always an agenda and a desire for position. Korah's motives were about position and the perceived glory that came with it, as Moses discerned. He lusted and coveted Aaron's position and he wanted it for himself. He was not satisfied with where the Lord had placed him. In the natural he could never be an Aaronic priest for he wasn't a descendant of Aaron, but Korah sought to find a way around this and promote himself to a position that God had never intended for him to have.

Korah had an incredibly blessed position, but it wasn't enough. Just like Satan was not satisfied with his position and sought to ascend to a position that wasn't his to have, so too was it with Korah. Even though Korah had a God given office, he wanted more and just like Satan, he corrupted others in an attempt to gain strength from numbers and get what he wanted.

Wherever the Lord places us to serve, for we are all called to serve not to rule, we have to serve with an attitude that we are serving unto the Lord. Our satisfaction must be derived from what we do for Him. If it is not, we will inevitably be dissatisfied for the flesh can never be satisfied by the service of the Spirit. The flesh looks for the recognition of the world and man and if it doesn't get it, it will look for a position where it thinks it will. This was the mistake of Satan and the same mistake of Korah. Our service has to be unto the Lord and our faith has to mirror that of king David's in trusting that if He wants us somewhere else, He will bring it to pass in His time (1 Sam 26:9-10).

A dissatisfaction of the flesh as to where the Lord has us serving may indicate that the spirit of Korah is present.

IF THERE IS BEHIND THE SCENES MURMURING.

The rebellion that we read of in Numbers 16 was not something that just happened overnight. From what is written, there is very clearly the key players of Korah, On, Dathan and Abiram and then seemingly a following of two hundred and fifty other Levites who were corrupted. This kind of momentum only happens when there are discussions! These men didn't all just have a spontaneous idea to rebel on the exact same day. This was something that had been talked about and talked out. Complaints and hurts were shared, and plans were formulated. Conspirators were recruited until the time came when the leaders believed they had enough followers and support to pull off the coup. This momentum was gained through behind the scenes murmurings. Korah, Dathan and Abiram didn't go to Moses and Aaron when it was just the three of them. They did not go and talk about their concerns and what they were feeling. The talked to others, behind the backs of Moses and Aaron, and they waited until they believed they had the strength of numbers. They sowed seeds of doubt over the leadership of Moses and Aaron and attracted those who had similar mindsets.

Murmurings are like fire. Fire needs three elements to survive: oxygen, heat and fuel. Removing one of these will see the fire slowly extinguish. Similarly, murmurings exist through three elements: an individual, complaints/hurts and a sympathetic and listening ear to hear them. Behind the scenes murmurings exist when we have an open ear to hear issues that an individual has with someone else. As believers we ever need to be aware of critical spirits and we must always operate in the biblical standard of going to our brother if we have a problem. These two things are safeguards that protect the people of God from murmurings. Whenever someone starts talking about their issues with someone else our first response should be, "have you spoken to them about it?"

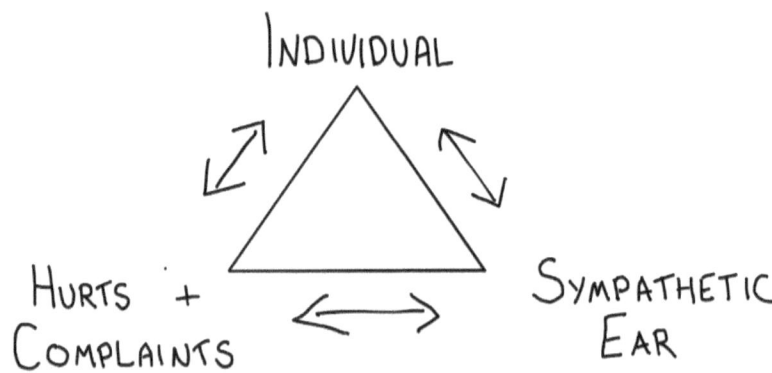

One of the things that we have to be aware of is that behind-the-scenes murmurings never reveal the fulness of the complaint or the agenda. They start off as seemingly innocent comments that may even be justifiable and relatable. But they are snowball like in affect. They build and build, and the critiques get more and more personnel. They are never done openly and are only ever shared with those whom they believe will be sympathetic. Any individuals that seemingly resist the invitation are shut off and shut out for fear that they may expose the discontent. These build and recruit until there is enough momentum and strength to publicly reveal the true agenda. When we as believers remove the fuel source of an open ear, we pour cold water on these sparks before they become a bush fire.

If there are murmurings about leadership at any level, then it may be a sign that the spirit of Korah is present.

IF THERE IS AN EVIDENT SUPERIORITY COMPLEX.

With both Cain and Balaam, we saw the effects of pride. With Korah we see an extension of this with the clear evidence of a superiority complex. Korah truly believed that he was better than Aaron.

When Korah arose against Moses and Aaron, Moses set forth that Korah and His followers should stand before the Lord with incense and Aaron would also stand before the Lord with incense. The one whom the Lord chose would be Holy and be his High Priest. Korah not only agrees to this and brings with him his two hundred and fifty followers with their incense, but he also gathers the entire congregation to witness what would happen. In Korah's mind the result was a foregone conclusion!

This clear arrogance rises to another level when we look back at Leviticus 10. Shortly after the consecration of the Tabernacle of Moses, two of the sons of Aaron, Nadab and Abihu were struck down by the Lord for presenting incense that the Lord had not commanded. The Lord had already shown that the presenting of incense was not a small thing. When done in a wrong way it brought about the judgement of the Lord. All of Israel would have been aware of this event and why it had happened and yet Korah did not blink when Moses instructed him to present incense before the Lord.

Korah not only thought that he was the better choice than Aaron he also presumed that this was how the Lord saw it. Such was his level of self-superiority that he believed that the Lord would show him to be His choice in front of the whole congregation. The pride associated with this superiority complex reveals such a deep level of self-deception within Korah. Korah's inflated views of himself actually robbed him of being able to serve the Lord in his God given office under the authority that the Lord had placed over him. This is really a culmination of the pride that we saw in Cain and with Balaam.

This same trait manifests itself when we wrongly believe that we are the preeminent experts in our fields, be it individually or corporately. We self-promote ourselves to positions that are not ours to have and at the same time we shut ourselves off from being able to receive input from those the Lord has placed over us. We can try to put others down so that we are exalted, and we take on the belief that the first should be the first. A superiority complex actually robs us of being able to have a teachable spirit and the ability to continue to grow as we believe that we have already made it. It will seek to cause us to step out of our God given positions and to seek that for which God never intended us to have.

A superiority complex is a clear sign that the spirit of Korah may be present.

IF THERE IS A REJECTION OF THE APOSTOLIC AND THE PROPHETIC.

Whilst we see with Korah's rebellion a rejection of the Godly ordained leadership for the nation of Israel, there is also more to it. The rejection that occurred was over the positions that the Lord had specifically given Aaron and Moses. Moses was the leader of Israel and Aaron was the appointed High Priest. As we read through the Old Testament, we unequivocally see Moses and Aaron in these roles. When we look at these two individuals through the lens of the New Testament though we see that Moses and Aaron were operating in what we would call the roles of Apostle and Prophet to the Church in the wilderness.

Moses was undoubtedly the spiritual leader for the Church in the wilderness. He was the man who met with God and brought His truth, revelation and teaching to the nation of Israel. He performed signs and miracles, raised up leaders and his successor. He oversaw the initiation and operation of the Tabernacle. Moses operated in the office of an apostle.

Aaron was given the role of the High Priest by the Lord. Aaron was in a sense the leader of the Tabernacle, with his sons under him and they oversaw the functioning and roles of the Tabernacle and the Levites who served there as priests. Aaron was Moses right hand man. If we look back in scripture though, we see that Aaron's service in the eyes of God was more than that of just a priestly office. When the Lord was calling Moses, we read:

So the LORD said to Moses: "See, I have made you as God to Pharaoh, **and Aaron your brother shall be your prophet.** *(Exo 7:1) NKJV*

Aaron was given the office of prophet by the Lord, and it was in this office that he supported the apostolic ministry of Moses. The Apostle and Prophet worked together in overseeing the Church in the wilderness.

This though was something that Korah wanted to change. One has to ask the question, what would have happened to Moses and Aaron if Korah and his followers had been successful? Would it have been just a quiet handover, or would Moses and Aaron have been banished from Israel or possibly even killed? One only has to look at the example of Absalom with his father David to see the intended outcomes of any positional challenge! (2 Sam 17) Korah's rebellion was not just a simple change of leadership; its purpose was to remove and kill the influence of the apostle and prophet. Korah and his followers wanted to be free of this influence and have the ability to operate under their own covering. They did not want the teachings and coverings that these offices brought; they wanted to be free to make their own choices.

What we see with Korah is a rejection of this apostolic and prophetic covering and a desire for autonomy. Korah sought to reject those who had been placed by the Lord into the positions of apostle and prophet. Korah as a Levitical priest operated in what we could call the role of pastor or teacher, and he was one who was not prepared to submit to the God given leadership that had been placed over him. He wanted to be the ceiling and did not want to operate under the God given leadership covering that existed. (1 Cor 12:28, Eph 4:11)

In our day, the spirit of Korah is evident when there is a rejection of the ministry of the apostle and prophet. We may well ask why does this happen? Why is there a rejection of these God given ministries? The apostle and prophet bring the truth of the Word of the Lord and correction to the people of God when they have strayed from it. They exist to lead and guide the Church and ensure that the Church is ready to be presented as the spotless bride she has been called to be. The truths and the correction that these two bring though will more often than not be counter to the beliefs and practices of the day and as such are met with hesitation, resistance and flat-out rejection. One only has to look at the history of Old Testament Israel to see the truth of this in the nation's responses to the prophets of their day. Rather than heeding the God given positions of the apostle and prophet and what they bring, they are rejected so that our own agendas can be pursued without resistance.

The office of apostle and prophet will be appointed, confirmed and testified too by the Lord. It is He who gives these spiritual offices unto man. They are not assumed positions, and neither are they achieved through a Christian promotional ladder. Men wrongly associate these offices with positions of prominence, but one only has to have a casual read through the New Testament to see that these are in fact positions of the greatest servitude. These offices are God given, exist for the benefit and building of the Church and as such need to be given the due respect by the people of God. (Eph 4:11)

Unfortunately, because of the world driven success mentality that we have in our modern thinking, like Korah there can be the temptation to aspire to positions that God never intended us to have. These positions can be wrongly associated with pride, standing and success. Korah as a Levite sought to be in a position that God never intended for him to be in. In modern day terms this same approach has the effect of setting a pastoral or teaching covering over the Church instead of the apostolic and prophetic covering God intended for it. Instead of seeing the God given blessing that these offices are, they can be seen as a threat to our position and standing and thus are rejected as a means of self-preservation. A rejection of these offices is really a rejection of Godly input and accountability. It is saying that we want to be the ones making decisions and in a sense be answerable to no one. As believers and Churches, we need to understand that just as with Korah, we are not rejecting men, but we are rejecting Godly ordained offices that He has given for the blessing, leading and growth of the people of God. This is the truth that Paul speaks of in 1 Corinthians 12. Just as Moses responded to Korah, "you are not rejecting Aaron but the Lord" (Num 16:11).

For those who are proven ministers in these offices, we as the people of God need to have an ear to hear what the Spirit is saying through them. Rather than be like Korah, we need to be open and respectful of these offices and heed the teachings and corrections that they may bring.

Where there is a blatant, unfounded rejection of the offices of apostles and prophet, particularly if it is just because what they say is contrary to how we want to do things, then it is an indicator that the spirit of Korah could be present.

Reflection

Like with our previous sections, below are some questions for us to ask ourselves and pray over as we consider the implications of the spirit of Korah.

- Am I satisfied in how I serve?

- Do I long for a different position or ministry?

- Am I prepared to wait on the Lord, or do I look for opportunities to make it happen?

- Do I speak negatively of leadership?

- Do I see myself as someone who has all the answers?

- Is my first response to go to the individual involved if I have a problem, offence etc?

- Do I listen and sympathise with the negative speech of others?

- How do we respond individually and corporately to the offices of apostle and prophet?

- Is the prophetic office evident in our Church or just the gift of prophecy?

- Are we open to the corrective words of apostles and prophets?

- Do we think that our way is the only way or the best way?

- How would we react if the Lord told us to do things differently?

- How are we with the thought of covering and accountability?

- Do we see ourselves as the answer for the Church?

Prayer

Lord, would you please search our hearts and reveal to us if any of these aspects of the spirit of Korah are present.

Where I have been dissatisfied with how I serve and the recognition I get from it would you please forgive me?

Where I have spoken or listened to negative talk surrounding leadership would you please forgive me?

Where I have knowingly or unknowingly rejected the God given ministries of apostle and prophet would you please speak and reveal this to me?

Lord, please remove any elements of this spirit and help me be ever mindful of its influence. Would you create in me a Godly humility and a passion to serve your Kingdom.

In Jesus' name.

Amen

Way
Error
Rebellion

Way → Error → Rebellion

Way Error Rebellion

Woe to them! For they have gone in the way of Cain, have run greedily in the error of Balaam for profit, and perished in the rebellion of Korah.(Jud 1:11) NKJV

Through this text we have taken time to consider the above quote from the book of Jude and to individually look at the three examples with in it and the three men that it refers to. We have then spent some time looking at the effects that these same three spirits seek to have on believers and the Church today.

As I was pondering the above, and that which we have so far discovered, I felt that what we have seen so far are not just three separate and distinct spirits that work in isolation, but rather three related spirits that work together in a cooperative sense and form a progressive path of destruction for the people of God. Jude in his writing didn't say that some of the individuals in question had gone in the way of Cain and others in the error of Balaam or that a third group followed in the rebellion of Korah. He very clearly stated that the individuals, the one group that were causing the discontent within the Church, had gone in the way of Cain, ran after the error of Balaam and perished in the rebellion of Korah. Jude was talking about a progressive path that was evident from the lives of these individuals. They had gone, they had run, and they had perished. In other words, there is a related and intertwined progression with these spirits. What we see from Jude's writing is that the spirit of Cain paves the way for the spirit of Balaam which in turn makes way for the spirit of Korah. It is a progressive path of Way, Error and Rebellion. These three spirits cooperate with a purpose to draw believers into a state of spiritual death, where the fires that once burned bright are left in a state of smouldering ashes as the Holy Spirit has been neglected and the flesh indulged.

Way → Error → Rebellion

Cain is the starting point for the effect of these spirits on believers and the Church as it sees the introduction of the flesh into our relationship with, our worship of and our approach unto the Lord. Just as with Cain it is the choice of a way. This spirit will seek to influence, but the choice is made by the individual or Church and if the way of Cain is chosen it is one that will lead to the error of Balaam and rebellion of Korah. With Cain we see an approach that sets aside the truth of the Word and instead seeks to approach the Lord in a way that is pleasing to the flesh. Cain was more focused on what pleased him in worship than on what pleased the Lord. Cain rejects the spiritual and focuses in on what satisfies man in their relationship with and worship of the Lord. It is a spirit of self-satisfaction and pride. It is an approach where the focus is not on the fire of God, but rather on what will please the crowd, what will attract and keep the multitude. The problem is that the satisfaction of the flesh will always draw a crowd. It will build a following and in the eyes of man it will appear to be successful. It will be bright, loud, attract the right people and from a worldly sense have all the hallmarks of success. Its appearance may be good, but it is a way that is devoid of the fire of God! It is a way that is rooted in self and works.

The way of Cain then opens the door for the spirit of Balaam. Having built a foundation based on flesh and pride with Cain, Balaam desperately seeks to not only hold onto this but grow it further with a focus on "worldly success", i.e. the gold and the glory. When the fire of God is not the hallmark of our lives and ministries, as with Cain, then the spirit of Balaam will seek to cause us to look to the success markers of the world (finance, recognition and numbers) in order to justify the success of our lives and ministries. It will encourage us to pursue these things in an ever-increasing measure for the flesh is never satisfied with where it currently stands. The flesh always wants more! This is what we saw with Balaam. There was a lack of satisfaction with what he had and a desperate pursuit for more. It was this pursuit with Balaam that saw compromise introduced to the people of God. The spirit of Balaam will seek to encourage the pursuit of the success markers of the world and cause the truths of the Word of God to be compromised and neglected for fear of impeding this. The spirit of Balaam would rather keep the status and financial success that has been built rather than risk losing them by preaching the truth. This approach can be religiously justified in any number of ways, but the fact of the matter is that, just as with Balaam, it is a focus on personal and corporate advancement at the expense of the advancement of the Kingdom **AND** at the expense of the advancement of the people of God. Balaam benchmarks worldly success as of most importance with little regard for the growth of the people in the things of God. It is success and growth based on the markers of the world not on the markers of God. Cain introduces the flesh, but Balaam pursues it further, running after it, with a lust for the benefits it can bring.

Finally, having chosen the way of Cain and then ran in the error of Balaam the spirit of Korah is evidenced when the Godly correction that comes through apostolic and prophetic ministries is rejected. The flesh that has been introduced through Cain, grows under Balaam and finally matures with Korah to the point that we are so steadfast in our ways that we have lost all sensitivity to the Holy Spirit's leading and correction. Godly leadership and authority are sought to be discarded as we reject those whom God has anointed and appointed and anything that does not align with our standard practices is rejected and often branded as religion just seeking to restrict our freedom. Korah's fruit comes from the seed that was sown it Cain. Under Korah the seed becomes a well-established tree and one that will not be easily moved.

What we have learned can be summarised by the following:

	SPIRIT OF CAIN
Way	*Cain looks for the satisfaction of the flesh in its relationship with the Lord even if it means being devoid of the fire of God. Its focus is on appealing to man more than the Lord. It will shut down the Spirit so that the flesh will be satisfied.*

⬇

	SPIRIT OF BALAAM
Error	*Balaam builds from the flesh and pride of Cain's approach and looks to the advancement of the individual or the individual Church at the expense of the advancement of the people of God and His Kingdom. It sees the introduction of compromise to the people of God in order for further personal or corporate benefit.*

⬇

	SPIRIT OF KORAH
Rebellion	*Finally, having its foundations firmly set in the flesh, Korah rejects any correction that comes through the apostolic and prophetic offices. The pride that was birthed with Cain is manifested here as the arrogance of Korah.*

Hopefully from this we can see the related progressive nature of these three spirits. The spirit of Cain aims to set the believer on a path that ends with the spirit of Korah. These spirits work together to slowly draw the believer and the Church further from the truths of the Word of God.

We also need to note the progressive actions of each spirit. What starts as a choice of path with the way of Cain, turns to running with the Spirit of Balaam. There is an increase in the momentum and traction with Balaam. It speeds the course and grows that which was birthed under Cain before finally leading to the last outcome, perishing with the spirit of Korah.

Gone → Run → Perished

What starts with Cain ends with Korah and in between there is a momentum that builds as we head towards the outcome of that path. In a negative sense it is the process of fruitfulness talked about by Jesus in Mark 4:28.

> *For the earth bringeth forth fruit of herself; first the blade, then the ear, after that the full corn in the ear. (Mar 4:28) KJV*

Jesus stated that it is first the blade, then the ear and then the corn. In this negative sense we see that the blade is Cain, the ear is Balaam and the corn is Korah. The blade comes from the planting of the seed, it is the first signs of life. The corn is the fruit, and once it is produced there is no denying what the seed was. In between though is the steady growth that comes through Balaam. Balaam grows from the seed of Cain and steadily matures with the goal of producing the fruit of Korah. It is first Cain, then Balaam and then Korah. It is a destructive spiritual progression, but each stage is dependent upon the one that precedes it.

Hopefully from the above we can see the progressive nature of both path and action of what we have been considering. We start in the way of Cain before running in the error of Balaam and finally perishing in the rebellion of Korah. It is ultimately a path of spiritual death. In contemplating the enormity of this and just what this passage from Jude reveals to us, we also need to mindful of several things:

1. That each of the men we have considered, Cain, Balaam and Korah were all individuals who had relationships with the Lord and served Him. These were not heathen or unbelieving individuals, but those who followed the Lord. One was offering a sacrifice, another was a prophet of the Lord and the third was a Levitical priest who handled the most holy articles of furniture in Moses Tabernacle.

2. When Jude wrote his message under the inspiration of the Holy Spirit, he was writing to a Church and the believers who were in it. This was not a letter to unbelievers, but those who were saved and attending Church. Jude was addressing a Church that had been

affected by these progressive spirits, and he was telling them as much.

> *Beloved, when I gave all diligence to write unto you of the common salvation, it was needful for me to write unto you, and exhort you that ye should earnestly contend for the faith which was once delivered unto the saints. For there are certain men crept in unawares, who were before of old ordained to this condemnation, ungodly men, turning the grace of our God into lasciviousness, and denying the only Lord God, and our Lord Jesus Christ. (Jud 1:3-4) KJV*

This was a letter imploring their eyes to be opened. Jude's plea was for the believing readers to take note of what he was saying and return to their foundational gospel truths. It was a call to address these spirits that had infiltrated and make an urgent course correction.

3. As the people of God, we need to be aware that the same spirits seek to come against the people of God today in order to hinder the advancement of the Kingdom of God. This message of Jude is part of all scripture which has been given by inspiration of God, and is profitable for doctrine, for reproof, for correction, for instruction in righteousness: (2Ti 3:16). We are in a real spiritual battle, and we need to be mindful of those things that would seek to hinder us. A little leaven leavens the whole lump. What can start seemingly small and innocuously with Cain will lead to a harvest with Korah just as it did with the Church Jude was writing to.

Jude's message is one that speaks to the Church and believers today warning us about these destructive spirits. These spirits work together and particularly target the Church and the people who comprise it with an intent of progressive destruction against the people of God. These three spirits cooperate and seek to progressively draw the people of God further and further away from the truth.

The Church at Laodicea

Interestingly enough, the book of Jude is not the only place in scripture where we see these three spirits working together and impacting a New Testament Church. In the book of Revelation, we read of Jesus addressing the spiritual state of seven New Testament Churches and in His comments to the Church at Laodicea we read:

> *"And to the angel of the church of the Laodiceans write, 'These things says the Amen, the Faithful and True Witness, the Beginning of the creation of God: "I know your works, that you are neither cold nor hot. I could wish you were cold or hot. So then, because you are lukewarm, and neither cold nor hot, I will vomit you out of My mouth. Because you say, 'I am rich, have become wealthy, and have need of nothing'—and do not know that you are wretched, miserable, poor, blind, and naked— I counsel you to buy from Me gold refined in the fire, that you may be rich; and white garments, that you may be clothed, that the shame of your nakedness may not be revealed; and anoint your eyes with eye salve, that you may see. As many as I love, I rebuke and chasten. Therefore be zealous and repent. Behold, I stand at the door and knock. If anyone hears My voice and opens the door, I will come in to him and dine with him, and he with Me. To him who overcomes I will grant to sit with Me on My throne, as I also overcame and sat down with My Father on His throne. (Rev 3:14-21) NKJV*

From this assessment of Jesus there are a few things for us to take note of in regard to the Church at Laodicea:

A FOCUS ON WORKS.

> ***"I know your works****, that you are neither cold nor hot. I could wish you were cold or hot. So then, because you are*

> ***lukewarm***, *and neither cold nor hot, I will vomit you out of My mouth. (Rev 3:15-16) NKJV*

Notice that Jesus doesn't say I know your faith! He says I know your **WORKS**! Cains approach to the Lord was based in the flesh through works. Cain approached with what he had toiled and worked hard for, and he presented these to the Lord as it satisfied him as a sacrifice. It was an approach based in works! Jesus makes a similar assessment of the Church at Laodicea; I know your works. He was literally saying "I am fully aware of that which you do" and that is where He left it. "I know", not "I am pleased" or "well done". Just "I know". You can almost hear the indifference in His voice as He says this.

Jesus then continued His assessment and told the Church that they were not hot or cold, but lukewarm. In other words, there had once been a fire burning, but it had been neglected and left to burn down. Similarly to Cain, the Church at Laodicea was also devoid of the fire of God. Faith produces fire, works do not! The pursuit of works had seen the fire of God neglected and the truth of this was evident in the spiritual state of the Church.

Laodicea had a focus on the works of the flesh and was devoid of the fire of God. The spirit of Cain was evident.

A FOCUS ON FINANCE.

> *Because you say,* ***'I am rich, have become wealthy, and have need of nothing'***—*and do not know that you are wretched, miserable, poor, blind, and naked— I counsel you to buy from Me gold refined in the fire, that you may be rich; and white garments, that you may be clothed, that the shame of your nakedness may not be revealed; and anoint your eyes with eye salve, that you may see. (Rev 3:17-18) NKJV*

Laodicea had a focus on the success markers of the world. They were rich, had become wealthy and had need of nothing. This was their testimony of themselves. Like Balaam, Laodicea had based their success on the markers of the world. They looked to the natural to determine how they stood as a Church and just like Balaam they were self-deceived. What they thought marked them as successful the Lord looked on with contempt. Whilst Laodicea looked at the natural, the Lord looked at the spiritual and saw that in reality they were actually "wretched, miserable, poor, blind and naked".

This was the early Church, built from the outpouring of the Lord in Acts 2 and yet we see the advancement of the people of God had been neglected for the pursuit of worldly success. These were not a people in a strong spiritual state. This was a Church in compromise that needed to be refined, clothed and have their eyes again opened. It was a Church where the spirit of Balaam was present. There was a focus on worldly success at the expense of the spiritual advancement of the people.

A LACK OF HEARING HIS VOICE.

> *As many as I love, I rebuke and chasten. Therefore be zealous and repent. Behold, I stand at the door and knock. If anyone hears My voice and opens the door, I will come in to him and dine with him, and he with Me. (Rev 3:19-20)* NKJV

Jesus came and said that because He loved them, He was rebuking them and chastening them. This was a word of correction that they needed to hear, to heed and then repent for how they had acted.

Jesus told them that He was standing at the door and knocking. He then goes further and says if any man hears my voice and opens the door, I will come in. In other words, Jesus wasn't just standing there and politely knocking, He was knocking and calling out to the Church for them to open the door unto Him. This was a Church made of up people who were followers of Jesus, but Jesus was saying that He had actually been relegated to the outside. He was knocking and calling, but so far, the Church had been unresponsive to His calls. Jesus was imploring them to have an ear to hear the corrective Word that was coming from Him through His apostle John.

Whilst Jesus was telling them that they have not heard His voice as He has been knocking, Laodicea's testimony of itself was that it needed nothing. Jesus wanted to be let in, Laodicea couldn't see that anything was wrong or missing. This call of Jesus was an imploration for the Church to be no longer closed off too His voice. They were to open the door that had been shut so that His voice would no longer be muffled, but rather clearly audible. Just as with Korah, we see with Laodicea that there was a lack of openness to any voice other than their own! The worldly success of the Church and the superiority complex this had given birth to had seen them lose the input of the voice of the Lord. Their voice had been magnified over His!

What we can see from the Church at Laodicea is summed up in the table below.

	SPIRITUAL TRAITS	**EVIDENCED AT LAODICEA**
SPIRIT OF CAIN	<ul><li>Approach by **works**.</li><li>A focus on the flesh and not the Spirit.</li><li>Lack of the fire of God.</li></ul>	<ul><li>Rev 3:15</li><li>Known for **works**.</li><li>Neither hot nor cold - no remaining fire. Lukewarm from the coals of what once had been.</li></ul>
SPIRIT OF BALAAM	<ul><li>Focus on the gold and the glory. Worldly markers of finance and success.</li><li>Not looking to Jehovah Jireh but seeing self as the provider.</li><li>Self-deception of our own righteousness through religious justifications.</li></ul>	<ul><li>Rev 3:17</li><li>I am rich – focus on mammon.</li><li>I have need of nothing - self provision.</li><li>Deceived over actual state.</li></ul>

SPIRIT OF KORAH	• Rejection of the corrective Words of God that come through the offices of apostle and prophet. • Seeking to be autonomous.	• Rev 3:19-20 • Jesus seeking to reprove and chasten the Church. • Spiritual door to the Church is currently shut and unresponsive to **His** voice and leading.

That which Jude had admonished his readers about was also alive and present in the Church at Laodicea. The spirits of Cain, Balaam and Korah can again be seen working together in the spiritual life of this Church. We again see the cooperative and progressive workings of these spirits. Note the progressive mentions of these spirits by Jesus:

Rev 3:15 – The spirit of Cain.

Rev 3:17 – The spirit of Balaam.

Rev 3:19-20 – The spirit of Korah.

Jesus progressively mentions the influences of these spirits as He examines His Church. These spirits work cooperatively to progressively lead believers and Churches down a path of spiritual death.

With Laodicea we see how these sprits have worked together in an effort to bring about the spiritual death of the Church. Jesus own words were that because of their lukewarmness, He was ready to spew them out of His mouth. What a sickening and gut-wrenching assessment this is by our Lord and Saviour over professed believers, but such speaks to their true spiritual state. What had started with the spirit of Cain sought to bring about the Church's spiritual death through the spirit of Korah.

As New Testament believers such should cause us to understand the reality of these spirits which seek to infiltrate and corrupt the Church. Just as they sought to corrupt the early church, so to do they seek to corrupt the Church today. To be forewarned is to be forearmed and it is my belief that the Lord is wanting His Church in this time to be aware of these spirits and where necessary, deal with those things that need to be dealt with.

As we have said, these spirits are progressive in nature and as such this path always starts with the way of Cain. It is the seeds of Cain the lead to the growth of Balaam and the fruit of Korah. Our greatest defence as the people of God is to be aware of this and be on guard for the seeds of Cain in our lives and Churches. These are the early warning signs and an indicator that we need to adjust our way to re-align with the truth.

Hopefully from what we have looked at, we have been able to see that these three spirits are cooperative and progressive. They work together, each making way for the other in an effort to ultimately bring about the spiritual death of the Church and the people of God who comprise it. Just as they sought to hinder the advancement of the early Church, so too are they active today seeking to lead the Church and believers down the path of Way, Error and Rebellion.

Way Truth Life

In this study we have looked at the Way of Cain, the Error of Balaam and the Rebellion of Korah. We have seen how these are cooperative spirits that form a progressive partnership to bring about spiritual death in the lives of believers and Churches. It is a path of spiritual destruction. It is the path of Way, Error and Rebellion.

Standing in complete contrast to what we have discovered in this text are the words of Jesus in the book of John, where we read:

> *And where I go you know, and the way you know." Thomas said to Him, "Lord, we do not know where You are going, and how can we know the way?" Jesus said to him,* ***"I am the way, the truth, and the life****. No one comes to the Father except through Me. (Joh 14:4-6) NKJV*

In response to Thomas' challenge of not knowing the way, Jesus said unto him "I am the Way, I am the Truth, and I am the Life". In this statement Jesus was outlining the path that believers are called to follow. It is again a progressive, cooperative path but this time it is one that brings about spiritual life. It is the path of Way, Truth and Life. It is a path of complete obedience unto the Word of the Lord, one that is Spirit led and unsullied by the flesh.

If we compare this verse in John and our quote from Jude what we see is two separate and distinct paths for believers to choose from:

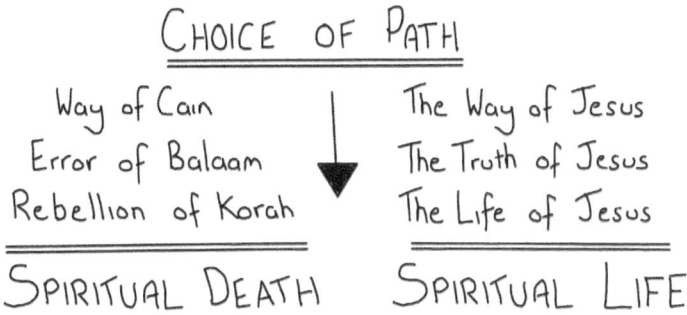

Our purpose here is not to do a study on the path of way, truth and life, for that is a study in itself, but rather to highlight that scripture reveals there is only two paths for us to follow. There is a path of way, error and rebellion and there is a path of way, truth and life. These two paths lead the believer and the Church in completely opposite directions. They are in fact as opposite as Cain and Abel for that is where the seeds of deviation began. Cain chose the way of works, introduced flesh into His approach unto the Lord and stepped away from the truth that the Lord had set forth. Cain heard and knew the truth, but he chose the way of disobedience. Abel though approached in faith, holding to the truth of the Word and acting in obedience unto it, worshipping the Lord in Spirit. Abel heard and obeyed. Both men had the choice of a path. Whereas Jude outlines for us the path of disobedience, Jesus in Mark tells believers that path of obedience. It is a call to fully, wholly and truly follow Him.

With every believer and every Church there lies a choice as to the path that we will take. We either make the choice of Abel or we make the choice of Cain. The choices we make though are more than just a way of approach, they are a choice of a path that we will journey on. It will either be a path that leads to spiritual life or one that will lead to spiritual death. With this we need to remember:

- That each of the men we looked at in this text had a relationship with the Lord and that both Jude and Jesus were addressing Churches and believers when they were detailing the issues associated with the spirits of Cain, Balaam and Korah. It would be arrogant of us to think that these same words do not serve as a warning to us as well or that we could not too be influenced by these spirits. It is the same kind of arrogance that was evident with Cain as he dictated to the Lord how he would approach!

- That the choice of path is not a onetime event that settles our journey forever. We have to always be able to reflect on our path to make sure we haven't strayed from it. How many times had Cain presented an acceptable sacrifice before he made the choice to present something different? The spirit of Cain is always seeking to pull the Church from the path of way, truth and life. It is a corrupting influence that seeks to infiltrate the bride and set us on the path of way, error and rebellion.

- The way of Cain never looks that drastically different to the way of Abel. Cain still approached the Lord, he still brought a sacrifice to Him, and he was still in relationship with Him. It is the subtle differences that make the way of Cain so dangerous. It is only as we hold to the foundational truths that Jude encourages us too that we can identify this spirits influence and guard ourselves from the path of way, error and rebellion.

As believers we ever need to be mindful of the spirits of Cain, Balaam and Korah and their effect on our lives and Churches. The greatest guard that we have is to be ever aware of the way we are walking in because the reality is that we are ever only on one of two ways.

> *"Enter by the narrow gate; for wide is the gate and* **broad is the way that leads to destruction***, and there are many who go in by it.* **Because narrow is the gate and difficult is the way which leads to life***, and there are few who find it. (Mat 7:13-14)* NKJV

We are either on the path of way, truth and life or the path of way, error and rebellion. The wide way of Cain will ever seek to plant the seed of flesh in our relationship with the Lord. It will seek to bring self into worship and cause us to deviate onto its path of way, error and rebellion. It is only through continual, prayerful and honest introspection with the guidance of the Holy Spirit that we can truly stay on the narrow way. It is the way in which we choose to walk that will determine whether we are on the path to spiritual life or the path to spiritual death. We must ever check the path that we are on and make sure that we are walking in the right way. Deviation can be subtle and if we are not continually checking our alignment to the way of Jesus we can easily end up off course in the way of Cain. It is only as we attend to the correct way that we can ensure that we are on the path to spiritual life.

May we always have the humble honesty to be led by the Holy Spirit as to our course and where needed correct it.

THE TWO HOUSES

The Two Houses

Whilst there is a level of application for all believers within this study, as I was writing this text, I very much felt that there was an impetus from the Lord for His Church in this season to grasp hold of the truths that have been presented. This text has been written with a focus largely on the Church. As I sought the Lord about this, I felt the Lord direct me to the parable of the wise of foolish builder found in Matt 7:24-27:

> *"Therefore whoever hears these sayings of Mine, and does them, I will liken him to a wise man who built his house on the rock: and the rain descended, the floods came, and the winds blew and beat on that house; and it did not fall, for it was founded on the rock. "But everyone who hears these sayings of Mine, and does not do them, will be like a foolish man who built his house on the sand: and the rain descended, the floods came, and the winds blew and beat on that house; and it fell. And great was its fall." (Mat 7:24-27) NKJV*

Whilst this is a parable we are all no doubt familiar with, I would encourage you to read over this parable a few times before moving forward. As we consider this parable, there are two things for us to take particular note of:

THE CENTRAL THEME OF THE PARABLE IS OBEDIENCE.

The rock in this parable is actually referring to obedience. The words of Jesus were that he who first of all **HEARS** and then second of all

DOES His words, i.e. he who acts in obedience, is like a wise man who built his house upon a rock. The rock here is the sure foundation that comes through acting in obedience to the Words of God.

This is contrasted to the foolish man who heard the exact same words, but didn't do them, i.e. he did not act in obedience to the Word. This person also built a house, but they didn't build in obedience but rather disobedience. This act of disobedience is compared to building on the sand.

The actions of the individuals in response to the words of Jesus is the focus here. The wise builder acted on Jesus Words and was obedient whereas the foolish builder was disobedient. When we build in obedience unto the Word of the Lord we build upon a sure foundation. Obedience is at the core of this parable.

THERE WERE TWO HOUSES.

Both the wise and the foolish built houses. There were two structures built. The progress of building was not inhibited by whether they built in obedience or disobedience. The difference between obedience and disobedience was evidenced in the foundations, but not in the structure! Both houses were constructed, finished and for a time both houses were standing together. There were two houses in existence.

I would suggest that this is a parable that has application to believers and Churches. Jesus was not addressing believers and non-believers here. He was speaking to those that are His and those that have heard His words. Both builders had ears to hear the words of the Lord. The houses that were built not only speak of our individual lives, but also the Church corporately for the Church is the house of God (1 Tim 3:15). Within the parable is a message of obedience that is needed in the lives of believers individually and corporately.

In the parable two houses were built and existed together.

Application to our Study

The building of the wise is done in obedience to the words of the Lord. It is a building process that follows the Lord's schematics. Just as Moses had to build the Tabernacle according to what was shown unto him, down to the finest detail so too is the New Testament Church to be built according to the instructions that the Lord has laid out in scripture. The Lord has laid out for how His house is to be built.

The foolish builder though, didn't build according to the Lord's commands. They heard the exact same instructions as the wise, but they chose a different path. They chose to build according to their own design just like Cain did. They heard and knew the Lord's design, but they chose to do things their own way.

Within this parable of Jesus, we see the truth of what we have discovered regarding the two paths. There is the path of Way, Truth and Life or there is the path of Way, Error and Rebellion. Each builder chose a path and the path he chose determined the outcome of the house. We again see the same progressive and cooperative process that we have discovered throughout this study:

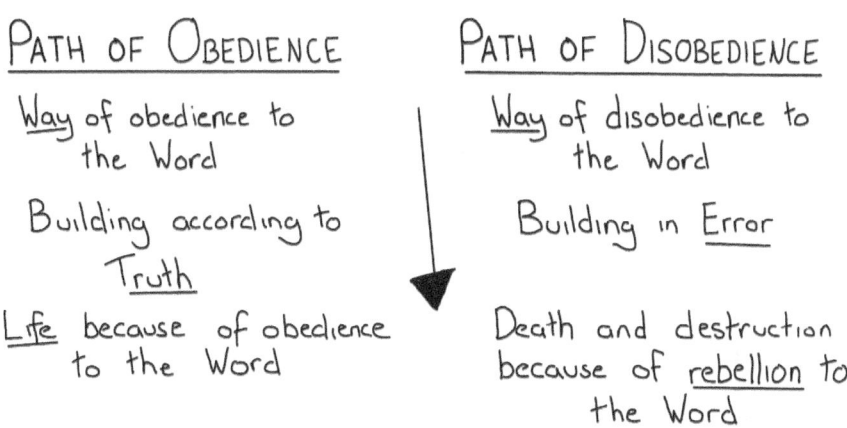

The wise and foolish builder further illustrate to us the paths of way, truth and life in contrast to that of way, error and rebellion and further reiterate to us that there are only ever two paths of approach. There is the right way or wrong way. The way of Abel or the way of Cain. The way of the wise builder or the way of the foolish.

The way which we chose to walk in will determine the ultimate outcome of either spiritual life or death for believers and Churches. Just as with Cain and Abel, the Wise and the Foolish builders both received the exact same instructions from the Lord and in both cases the deviation in ways came through a choice to either be obedient or disobedient unto the Word of the Lord. It is the choice of path that determines our outcome.

Diving Deeper

What we have looked at so far should fit with most of our existing understanding of this parable. The particular impetus that I felt though surrounds that which came against the houses to test them. The two houses were both built and in existence at the same time and the exact same elements come against both houses. I have always been taught and heard the interpretations of the rain, winds and storm from a negative point of view. They are the false doctrines, the things of the world which come against believers and the Church and the storms of life that come to test and try the house. These will ultimately cause the houses destruction if it has not been built on the rock of obedience.

I would not disagree with this at all, but as I was meditating upon this parable, I was struck by the thought, "what if these things were also from a positive perspective in the parable?" What if the rains, flood and wind had a positive connotation? Let's take a moment to briefly consider each of these elements:

WIND.

In scripture we understand that the wind is symbolic of the Holy Spirit. Jesus alludes to this in His discourse with Nicodemus and we see in Acts 2 at the birth of the Church that the wind of the Spirit comes and fills the house just before the tongues of fire descended on those that were gathered there.

RAINS.

From Joel 2 and James 5 we understand that the rains upon the earth are symbolic of outpourings of the Holy Spirit, particular those of the last days. See also Zech 10:1.

FLOODS, RIVER.

The Greek word used for flood means "a *current, brook* or *freshet* (as *drinkable*), that is, *running water" and is translated as* "flood, river, stream, water"

Ezekiel 47 speaks of a river of life that flows from the throne of God. This river speaks of a life of immersion that believers are called to have in the Spirit. It is a river that keeps deeper and deeper that more that we press in!

What if the wind, rain and waters of the parable speak not just in a negative sense of things that come against believers and Churches? What if they speak of the outpourings of the Holy Spirit that the Lord is going to bless us with? What if they speak of that which the Lord is going to outpour upon His people in these days?

My belief is that there is such an incredible move of God coming that it is going to shake every believer and every Church. The wind, rain and rivers of the Spirit are not designed to bring destruction, but to see an incredible move of the Holy Spirit like never before. For Churches and individuals to be able to house what God is going to do though, they must be like the wise builder and chose the path of obedience. It is only upon choosing the path of Way, Truth and Life that individuals and Churches will be able to stand when the Lord unleashes the magnitude of this outpouring. Why? Because these have followed the Word of the Lord and in obedience built according to the Lord's specifications. They have followed the plans which means that they have the structural integrity to be able to house that which the Lord is going to do.

As an illustration, let's consider for a moment a fish tank that you can buy from any pet store in varying sizes and take home. You can set up a thriving tank with fish that looks amazing and keeps the kids entertained. The filter cleans the water, the glass and seals contain the water, and the fish get feed. Everything works. If you were to build a massive aquarium though, one capable of holding sharks and large fish where tourists could come and explore the marvels of the sea you wouldn't use the same glass as you would for a home aquarium. You would need glass that was much thicker and stronger. In fact, you would need glass of a certain specification to be able to handle the weight and pressure of what was going to fill it. The aquarium couldn't be built with just any materials. Everything would have to meet the design specifications that had been deemed necessary in order for them to contain what it was intended to contain.

It is the exact same thing with the Church. God has laid out in His Word the exact specifications for our lives and Churches to be able to handle that which He wants to pour in. The truths seen in the specifications of the Old Testament Tabernacle of Moses foreshadow this New Testament truth. God's Word provides us with His blueprint for our lives individually and corporately. It is only when we choose the path of obedience and build according to **HIS TRUTH** though that we become capable of holding that which He wants to infill us with. When we build in error, having strayed from the truth, we are like an aquarium with inferior glass. We are unable to hold that which He wants to pour in and like the foolish man's house, destruction will result. We literally come apart at the seams as we do not have the foundational strength to hold the weight of what He is wanting to do.

It is my belief that God is calling His Son's bride corporately and individually to be ready for that which He is wanting to do. He is calling us all to examine our ways. This is not a quick checklist of items, but rather a time of Spirit lead introspection to look at whether we are walking in the path of way, truth and life or the path of way, error and rebellion. It is time for us to look, reflect, repent and correct our course. We are in a season of preparation and if we truly want to be ready for what He is going to do we need to prepare now. We need to remove those things of the spirit of Cain, Balaam and Korah and in complete and full obedience seek the Lord.

The call now is for the Church and His people to be wise builders. It is a season of preparation for what is to come. Now is the time to address any things that need to be addressed and make sure that we are building according to the specifications of truth. It is time for the Church to check its course!

Final Comments

The preparation of this text is something that has challenged, stretched and grown me. It has forced me to look at areas I had not considered before and at times to repent of areas where I had strayed from the path of way, truth and life and onto that of way, error and rebellion.

It is my sincere prayer that you have received something from the Lord as you have read through the pages of this text. I feel that in our time there is an ever-increasing call of the Lord for purity in the bride of His Son. He is calling, He is leading, and He is correcting so that we may be ready for that which He is about to do. As the people of God, we ever need to be aware of the spirits of Cain, Balaam and Korah and their desire to cause us to stray from the true path. We ever need to have our Holy Spirit led navigational compass out to ensure that we remain on the true way.

The path of obedience is not always popular, but it always leads to life! May it be one that we always choose.

> *I call heaven and earth as witnesses today against you, that I have set before you life and death, blessing and cursing;* **therefore choose life**, *that both you and your descendants may live; (Deu 30:19) NKJV*

Choose Life!

Blessing in Christ,

Courtney

Bibliography

- The Authorised King James version of the Bible, Public Domain.
- Scriptures takes from the New King James Version. Copyright ©1982 by Thomas Nelson, Inc. Used by permission. All rights reserved
- Strong, James. The New Strong's Expanded Exhaustive Concordance of the Bible. Thomas Nelson, 2010
- Laird, C.A. In Spirit and In Truth, *The Call of True Worship*.

Other Texts by the Author

If my people, which are called by my name, shall humble themselves, and pray, and seek my face, and turn from their wicked ways; then will I hear from heaven, and will forgive their sin, and will heal their land. (2Ch 7:14)

In 2 Chronicles we read of the temple of the Lord being built by King Solomon after many years of planning and preparation by King David. Just after the Temple's dedication, we read in 2 Chronicles 7:11-16 that the Lord spoke to Solomon through a dream. It is the words of the Lord to Solomon in this dream that form the basis of this study. As we examine this dialogue, we discover that there are a number of biblical truths that flow from this encounter.

If My People examines what these truths are and follows them through scripture before considering their application to the Church. The call of the Lord in 2 Chronicles is one that echoes to the Church of today. The precedent that the Lord set forth to Solomon has application to us as believers. Within the pages of this study we well discover how the call of "If My People" applies to the Church of today and the responsibilities that come with it. The Lord has much for His Church and His people if they can fulfill His call of "If My People'.

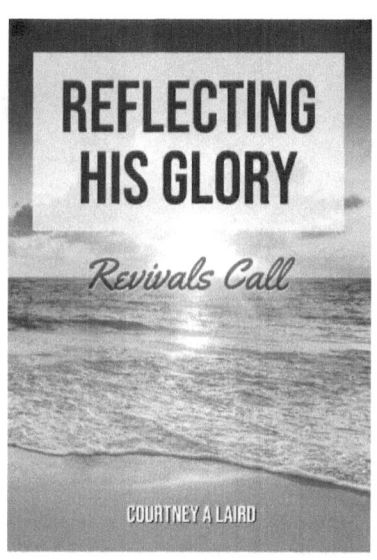

Were we made to reflect His Glory? How do we shine in a world that seems so dark? What is Revivals Call?

This text considers the call that exists within scripture for believers individually and corporately as the Church, to shine and reflect the glory of the Lord in the areas where He has planted them. As we investigate this call, we see that there is not only an onus on believers and churches to shine, but there is also a process laid out in scripture for how this occurs. The Lord not only calls us to shine, He shows us how to fulfill this call! Through examining this process, we learn not only how we reflect His glory and shine, but also what is seen when we do and ultimately what happens to the world around us when we reflect the glory of the Lord brightly.

It is the my belief that we are in a time when the Lord is stirring His people and His Church to shine as brightly as they have been called to. There is a call of the Lord unto His people in this day. It is Revivals Call. The Lord is calling His people to a new depth of relationship, one where we will reflect His glory as brightly as we have been called to. If we will respond to this call of revival, then we will see the Lord move in mighty ways and His kingdom will advance in the areas where we live.

THE CALL OF
TRUE WORSHIP

IN SPIRIT AND IN TRUTH

COURTNEY LAIRD

In John chapter 4 we read of an encounter between Jesus and a Samaritan woman at the well of Jacob. As the conversation transpires, we see the theme move from thirst to Worship and in a few concise verses Jesus expounds to the Samaritan woman the type of worship that the Father was seeking from His people.

Our purpose in this text is to examine the words of Jesus in these verses and consider how they apply today. How do we individually and corporately be the kind of the worshippers that Jesus spoke of? What does it mean to worship in spirit and in truth and how do we know if we are fulfilling this call?

I believe that we are in a season when the Lord is calling His people back to the truths of His Word and part of that call involves making sure that our worship aligns with what He has called us to offer. In this season there is an invitation from the Father for His people to go deeper and it is my prayer that this text may help you on that journey.

www.ingramcontent.com/pod-product-compliance
Lightning Source LLC
Chambersburg PA
CBHW031254290426

44109CB00012B/574